Social Skills Activities for the Elementary Grades

Dianne Schilling

Susanna Palomares

Copyright © 2016, INNERCHOICE PUBLISHING • All rights reserved

ISBN-10: 1-56499-094-X

ISBN-13: 978-1-56499-094-5

Student experience sheets may be reproduced in quantities sufficient for distribution to students in groups utilizing Social Skills Activities for the Elementary Grades. All other reproduction for any purpose whatsoever is explicitly prohibited without written permission. Requests for permission may be directed to INNERCHOICE PUBLISHING.

INNERCHOICE Publishing
15079 Oak Chase Court
Wellington, FL 33414

(561) 790-0132 • (561) 753-8620 Fax
www.InnerchoicePublishing.com

Contents

Introduction 1

Leading Sharing Circles 5

Activity Units

    Positive Self-talk 15

    Making Positive Choices 27

    Communicating Effectively 39

    Being Responsible 59

    Following Rules 71

    Understanding Body Language 81

    Making and Keeping Friends 93

    Cooperating With Others 109

    Helping Others 121

    Appreciating Differences 133

    Managing Anger and Fear 151

    Managing Conflict 161

Introduction

Relating effectively to others is a challenge we all face. People who are effective in their social interactions have the ability to understand others. They know how to interact flexibly, skillfully, and responsibly. At the same time, they recognize their own needs and maintain their own integrity. Socially effective people can process the nonverbal as well as verbal messages of others. They possess the very important awareness that all people have the power to affect one another. They are aware of not only how others affect them, but the effects their behaviors have on others.

In order to build healthy relationships, children need to have positive interpersonal experiences and to gain information concerning the social realm of life. As a rule, we do not systematically teach children how to understand and get along with other people. However, since social skills are fundamental to success in life, and are learned behaviors, children should be consistently and developmentally taught these important skills.

It is important to recognize that people who enjoy effective social relationships are exhibiting not just one ability, but many different skills, each at a different level of development with different nuances of understanding.

The activities and Sharing Circles in this book are designed to help children become aware of the importance of effectively relating to others, and to teach them social interaction skills in a deliberate and enjoyable fashion. Each of the twelve instructional units addresses a specific area of skill development. Initial units focus on self-awareness, which is fundamental to understanding and relating well to others.

Each unit contains two Sharing Circles, this book's primary vehicle for teaching social skills to children. In addition, group activities provide children with experiences that allow them to explore interpersonal relations from many angles and through many learning styles. Discussion questions are an integral part of each activity, and encourage children to consider and internalize what they have learned.

How Sharing Circles Teach Social Skills

The Sharing Circle process has been designed so that healthy, responsible behaviors are modeled by the teacher or counselor in his or her role as circle leader. The rules also require that the children relate positively and effectively to one another. The Sharing Circle brings out and affirms the positive qualities inherent in everyone and allows children to practice effective modes of communication. Through regular practice and reinforcement, children internalize effective interpersonal skills and are then able to transfer those skills to other situations. Because Sharing Circles provide a place where participants are listened to and their feelings accepted, children learn how to provide the same conditions to peers and adults outside the circle.

One of the great benefits of the Sharing Circle is that it does not merely teach young people about social interaction, it lets them interact! Every Sharing Circle is a real-life experience of social interaction where the children share, listen, explore, plan, dream, and problem solve together. As they interact, they learn about each other and they realize what it takes to relate effectively to others. Any given Sharing Circle may provide a dozen tiny flashes of positive interpersonal insight for an individual participant. Gradually, the reality of what constitutes effective behavior in relating to others is internalized.

Through this regular sharing of interpersonal experiences, the children learn that behavior can be positive or negative, and sometimes both at the same time. Consequences can be constructive, destructive, or both. Different people respond differently to the same event. They have different feelings and thoughts. The children begin to understand what will cause what to happen; they grasp the concept of cause and effect; they see themselves affecting others and being affected by others.

The ability to make accurate interpretations and responses in social interactions, when combined with growing self-knowledge and awareness, produces a broad and practical sense of values or ethics. When children possess this ability, they know where they stand with themselves and with others. They can tell what actions "fit" a situation. Sharing Circles are marvelous testing grounds where children can observe themselves and others in action, and can begin to see themselves as contributing to the good and bad feelings of others. With this understanding, children are helped to conclude that being responsible towards others feels good, and is the most valuable and personally rewarding form of interaction.

4

Leading Sharing Circles

This section is a thorough guide for conducting Sharing Circles. It covers major points to keep in mind and answers questions which will arise as you begin using the program. Please remember that these guidelines are presented to assist you, not to restrict you. Follow them, and trust your own leadership style at the same time.

The Sharing Circle is a structured communication process that provides students a safe place for learning about life and developing important aspects of social-emotional learning.

First, we'll provide a brief overview of the process of leading a Sharing Circle and then we'll cover each step in more detail.

A Sharing Circle begins when a group of students and the adult leader sit down together in a circle so that each person is able to see the others easily. The leader of the Sharing Circle briefly greets and welcomes each individual, conveying a feeling of enthusiasm blended with seriousness.

When everyone appears comfortable, the leader takes a few moments to review the Sharing Circle Rules. These rules inform the students of the positive behaviors required of them and guarantees the emotional safety and security, and equality of each member.

After the students understand and agree to follow the rules, the leader announces the topic for the session. A brief elaboration of the topic follows in which the leader provides examples and possibly mentions the topics relationship to prior topics or to other things the students are involved in. Then the leader re-states the topic and allows a little silence during which circle members may review and ponder their own related memories and mentally prepare their verbal response to the topic. (The topics and elaborations are provided in this curriculum.)

Next, the leader invites the circle participants to voluntarily share their responses to the topic, one at a time. No one is forced to share, but everyone is given an opportunity to share while all the other circle members listen attentively. The circle participants tell the group about themselves, their personal experiences, thoughts, feelings, hopes and dreams as they relate to the topic. Most of the circle time is devoted to this sharing phase because of its central importance.

During this time, the leader assumes a dual role—that of leader and participant. The leader makes sure that everyone who wishes to speak is given the opportunity while simultaneously enforcing the rules as necessary. The leader also takes a turn to speak if he or she wishes.

After everyone who wants to share has done so, the leader introduces the next phase of the Sharing Circle by asking several discussion questions. This phase represents a transition to the intellectual mode and allows participants to reflect on and express learnings gained from the sharing phase and encourages participants to combine cognitive abilities and emotional experiencing. It's in this phase that participants are able to crystallize learnings and to understand the relevance of the discussion to their daily lives. (Discussion questions for each topic are provided in this curriculum.)

When the students have finished discussing their responses to the questions and the session has reached a natural closure, the leader ends the session. The leader thanks the students for being part of the Sharing Circle and states that it is over.

What follows is a more detailed look at the process of leading a Sharing Circle.

Steps for Leading a Sharing Circle
1. Welcome Sharing Circle members
2. Review the Sharing Circle rules *
3. Introduce the topic
4. Sharing by circle members
5. Ask discussion questions
6. Close the circle

*optional after the first few sessions

1. Welcome Sharing Circle members

As you sit down with the students in a Sharing Circle group, remember that you are not teaching a lesson. You are facilitating a group of people. Establish a positive atmosphere. In a relaxed manner, address each student by name, using eye contact and conveying warmth. An attitude of seriousness blended with enthusiasm will let the students know that this Sharing Circle group is an important learning experience—an activity that can be interesting and meaningful.

2. Review the Sharing Circle rules

At the beginning of the first Sharing Circle, and at appropriate intervals thereafter, go over the rules for the circle. They are:

> **Sharing Circle Rules**
> - Everyone gets a turn to share, including the leader.
> - You can skip your turn if you wish.
> - Listen to the person who is sharing.
> - There are no interruptions, probing, put-downs, or gossip.
> - Share the time equally.

From this point on, demonstrate to the students that you expect them to remember and abide by the ground rules. Convey that you think well of them and know they are fully capable of responsible behavior. Let them know that by coming to the Sharing Circle they are making a commitment to listen and show acceptance and respect for the other students and you. It is helpful to write the rules on chart paper and keep them on display for the benefit of each Sharing Circle session.

3. Introduce the topic

State the topic, and then in your own words, elaborate and provide examples as each lesson in this book suggests. The introduction or elaboration of the topic is designed to get students focused and thinking about how they will respond to the topic. By providing more than just the mere statement of the topic, the elaboration gives students a few moments to expand their thinking and to make a personal connection to the topic at hand. Add clarifying statements of your own that will help the students understand the topic. Answer questions about the topic, and emphasize that there are no "right" responses. Finally, restate the topic, opening the session to responses (theirs and yours). Sometimes taking your turn first helps the students understand the aim of the topic. The introductions, as written in this book, are provided to give you some general ideas for opening the Sharing Circle. It's important that you adjust and modify the introduction and elaboration to suit the ages, abilities, levels, cultural/ethnic backgrounds and interests of your students.

4. Sharing by circle members

The most important point to remember is this: The purpose of these Sharing Circles is to give students an opportunity to express themselves and be accepted for the experiences, thoughts, and feelings they share. Avoid taking the action away from the students. They are the stars!

5. Ask discussion questions

Responding to discussion questions is the cognitive portion of the process. During this phase, the leader asks thought-provoking questions to stimulate free discussion and higher-level thinking. Each Sharing Circle lesson in this book concludes with several discussion questions. At times, you may want to formulate questions that are more appropriate to the level of understanding in your students—or to what was actually shared in the circle. If you wish to make connections between the topic and your content area, ask questions that will accomplish that objective and allow the answering of the discussion questions to extend longer. We have left a space on each page for you to note significant other questions that you create and find effective.

6. Close the circle

The ideal time to end a Sharing Circle is when the discussion question phase reaches natural closure. Sincerely thank everyone for being part of the circle. Don't thank specific students for speaking, as doing so might convey the impression that speaking is more appreciated than mere listening. Then close the group by saying, "This Sharing Circle is over," or "OK, that ends our circle."

More about Sharing Circle Steps and Rules

The next few paragraphs offer further clarification concerning leadership of Sharing Circles.

Who gets to talk? Everyone. The importance of acceptance cannot be overly stressed. In one way or another practically every ground rule says one thing: accept one another. When you model acceptance of students, they will learn how to be accepting. Each individual in the group is important and deserves a turn to speak if he or she wishes to take it. Equal opportunity to become involved should be given to everyone in the Sharing Circle.

Members should be reinforced equally for their contributions. There are many reasons why a leader may become more enthused over what one student shares than another. The response may be more on target, reflect more depth, be more entertaining, be philosophically more in keeping with one's own point of view, and so on. However, students need to be given equal recognition for their contributions, even if the contribution is to listen silently throughout the session.

In most of the Sharing Circles, plan to take a turn and address the topic, too. Students usually appreciate it very much and learn a great deal when their teachers, counselors, and other adults are willing to tell about their own experiences, thoughts, and feelings. In this way you let your students know that you acknowledge your own humanness.

Does everyone have to take a turn? No. Students may choose to skip their turns. If the circle becomes a pressure situation in which the members are coerced in any way to speak, it will become an unsafe place where participants are not comfortable. Meaningful discussion is unlikely in such an atmosphere. By allowing students to make this choice, you are showing them that you accept their right to remain silent if that is what they choose to do.

As you begin the circle, it's important to remember that it's not a problem if one or more students decline to speak. If you are imperturbable and accepting when this happens, you let them know you are offering them an opportunity to experience something you think is valuable, or at least worth a try, and not attempting to force-feed them. You as a leader should not feel compelled to share a personal experience in every session, either. However, if you decline to speak in most of the sessions, this may have an inhibiting effect on the students' willingness to share.

Some leaders ask the participants to raise their hands when they wish to speak, while others simply allow free verbal sharing without soliciting the leader's permission first. Choose the procedure that works best for you, but do not call on anyone unless you can see signs of readiness. And do not merely go around the circle.

Some leaders have reported that their first group fell flat—that no one, or just one or two students, had anything to say. But they continued to have groups, and at a certain point everything changed. Thereafter, the students had a great deal to say that these leaders considered worth waiting for. It appears that in these cases the leaders' acceptance of the right to skip turns was a key factor. In time most students will contribute verbally when they have something they want to say, and when they are assured there is no pressure to do so.

Sometimes a silence occurs during a session. Don't feel you have to jump in every time someone stops talking. During silences students have an opportunity to think about what they would like to share or to contemplate an important idea they've heard. A general rule of thumb is to allow silence to the point that you observe group discomfort. At that point move on. Do not switch to another topic. To do so implies you will not be satisfied until the students speak. If you change to another topic, you are telling them you didn't really mean it when you said they didn't have to take a turn if they didn't want to.

If you are bothered about students who attend a number of sessions and still do not share verbally, reevaluate what you consider to be involvement. Participation does not necessarily mean talking. Students who do not speak are listening and learning.

How can I encourage effective listening? The Sharing Circle is a time (and place) for students and leaders to strengthen the habit of listening by doing it over and over again. No one was born knowing how to listen effectively to others. It is a skill like any other that gets better as it is practiced. In the immediacy of the Sharing Circle the members become keenly aware of the necessity to listen, and most students respond by expecting it of one another.

In these Sharing Circles, listening is defined as the respectful focusing of attention on individual speakers. It includes eye contact with the speaker and open body posture. It eschews interruptions of any kind. When you lead a circle, listen and encourage listening in the students by (l) focusing your attention on the person who is speaking, (2) being receptive to what the speaker is saying (not mentally planning your next remark), and (3) recognizing the speaker when she finishes speaking, either verbally ("Thanks, Shirley") or nonverbally (a nod and a smile).

To encourage effective listening in the students, reinforce them by letting them know you have noticed they were listening to each other and you appreciate it.

How can I ensure the students get equal time? When group members share the time equally, they demonstrate their acceptance of the notion that everyone's contribution is of equal importance. It is not uncommon to have at least one dominator in a group. This person is usually totally unaware that by continuing to talk he or she is taking time from others who are less assertive. An important social skill is knowing how you affect others in a group and when dominating a group is inappropriate behavior.

Be very clear with the students about the purpose of this ground rule. Tell them at the outset how much time there is. When it is your turn, always limit your own contribution. If someone goes on and on, do intervene (dominators need to know what they are doing), but do so as gently and respectfully as you can.

What are some examples of put-downs? Put-downs convey the message, "You are not okay as you are." Some put-downs are deliberate, but many are made unknowingly. Both kinds are undesirable in a Sharing Circle because they destroy the atmosphere of acceptance and disrupt the flow of sharing and discussion. Typical put-downs include:
- over questioning.
- statements that have the effect of teaching or preaching
- advice giving
- one-upsmanship
- criticism, disapproval, or objections
- sarcasm
- statements or questions of disbelief

How can I deal with put-downs? There are two major ways for dealing with put-downs: preventing them from occurring and intervening when they do.

Going over the rules with the students at the beginning of each Sharing Circle, particularly in the earliest sessions, is a helpful preventive technique. Another is to reinforce the students when they adhere to the rule. Be sure to use non patronizing, non evaluative language.

Unacceptable behavior should be stopped the moment it is recognized by the leader. When you become aware that a put-down is occurring, do whatever you ordinarily do to stop destructive behavior. If one student gives another an unasked-for bit of advice, say for example,

"Jane, please give Alicia a chance to tell her story." To a student who interrupts say, "Ed, it's Sally's turn." In most cases the fewer words, the better—students automatically tune out messages delivered as lectures.

Sometimes students disrupt the group by starting a private conversation with the person next to them. Touch the offender on the arm or shoulder while continuing to give eye contact to the student who is speaking. If you can't reach the offender, simply remind him or her of the rule about listening.

If students persist in putting others down or disrupt the circle, ask to see them at another time and hold a brief one-to-one conference, urging them to follow the rules. Suggest that they reconsider their membership in the group. Make it clear that if they don't intend to honor the rules, they are not to come to the group.

How can I keep students from gossiping? Periodically remind students that using names and sharing embarrassing information in a Sharing Circle is not acceptable. Urge the students to relate personally to one another, but not to tell intimate details of their lives.

What should the leader do during the discussion question phase? Conduct this part of the process as an open forum, giving students the opportunity to discuss a variety of ideas and accept those that make sense to them. Don't impose your opinions on the students, or allow the students to impose theirs on one another. Ask open-ended questions, encourage higher-level thinking, contribute your own ideas when appropriate, and act as a facilitator.

In Conclusion: The Two Most Important Things to Remember

No matter what happens in a Sharing Circle session, the following two elements are the most critical:

1. Everyone gets a turn.
2. Everyone who takes a turn gets listened to with respect.

What does it mean to get a turn? Imagine a pie divided into as many pieces as there are people in the group. Telling the students that everyone gets a turn, whether they want to take it or not, is like telling them that each one gets a piece of the pie. Some students may not want their piece right away, but they know it's there to take when they do want it. As the teacher or counselor, you must protect this shared ownership. Getting a turn not only represents a chance to talk, it is an assurance that every member of the group has a "space" that no one else will violate.

When students take their turn, they will be listened to. There will be no attempt by anyone to manipulate what a student is offering. That is, the student will not be probed, interrupted, interpreted, analyzed, put-down, joked-at, advised, preached to, and so on. To "listen to" is to respectfully focus attention on the speaker and to let the speaker know that you have heard what he or she has said.

In the final analysis, the only way that a Sharing Circle can be evaluated is against these two criteria. Thus, if only two students choose to speak, but are listened to—even if they don't say very "deep" or "meaningful" things—the discussion group can be considered a success.

Positive Self-talk

As we respond to the people and events in our lives, we hear our own voices. Unfortunately, too much of what we hear is negative and discouraging. Since positive self-esteem is built with an "I can" attitude, and since positive attitudes and esteem are indicators of how well people get along with and understand others, it is important that the messages we give ourselves be encouraging—not discouraging. The more children can learn to be their own encouragers, the greater their chances for success in all areas. This unit offers children a variety of opportunities to transform negative self-talk to positive self-talk, and to consciously give themselves encouraging words.

A Time I Knew I Could Do It

A Sharing Circle

Directions:

Introduce the topic: *Our topic for this session is, "A Time I Knew I Could Do It."*

Elaborate: *Sometimes we just know we can do something. We don't doubt it at all. Think of a time when you felt confident that you could do something. It might have been that you knew you could master a new dance step, pass a test, sink a basket, or get your room clean before you went to the movies. It could have been something quick and easy that required limited effort, or something more difficult. Whatever it was, you knew you could do it—and you were right. Take a few moments to think it over, and remember, "A Time I Knew I Could Do It."*

You might want to share first this time. Then invite the children to take turns speaking. Listen carefully, and thank each person for sharing. Don't allow negative interruptions.

Discussion Questions:

After each child who wants to speak has done so, ask the children:
— How did you know that you could do the thing you shared?
— Do you think you could do the same thing again? Why or why not?

I Succeeded Because I Encouraged Myself

A Sharing Circle

Directions:

Introduce the topic: *Our topic for this session is, "I Succeeded Because I Encouraged Myself."*

Elaborate: *Have you ever wanted to do something and weren't quite sure you could? Think of a time when you felt unsure, but encouraged yourself and, consequently, found a way to be successful. Perhaps you tried to teach your pet a trick, or needed to do a good job on a report for school. Maybe you were trying to master something on a computer, or were learning a new game. Whatever it was, you were not sure you could do it, but after giving yourself some encouraging words, you were successful. Take a few quiet moments to think it over. The topic is, "I Succeeded Because I Encouraged Myself."*

Invite the children to take turns speaking. Make sure there are no negative interruptions. Listen attentively and thank each child for sharing. Be sure to take a turn yourself.

Discussion Questions:

After every child who wants to speak has done so, ask the children:
— What do you think caused each of you to be successful?
— What kinds of doubts did you have to overcome to be successful?
— What do you think would have happened if you had used discouraging words instead of encouraging words?

I'll Have to Hand It to You

Identifying and Sharing Positive Attributes

Materials:

Paper and pencils

Directions:

Make sure all the children have paper and a pencil. Ask the children to trace their hand in the middle of the paper and to write their names inside the palm area.

Instruct the children to label their thumb and fingers as follows (you may want to write these directions on the board to allow the children time to reflect on each item.):
— On the thumb write down something you are good at doing.
— On the index finger write down something that you enjoy doing.
— On the middle finger write down something you haven't done yet but would like to do someday.
— On the ring finger write down something you would like to improve about yourself.
— On the pinky finger write down something you are proud of.

When the children finish the writing assignment, have them move around the room with their completed hand prints. Within the allotted time you choose, tell the children to interact with as many other children as possible to share one item they wrote down. When the children have "connected" and "shared" with most, or all the others, ask these and other of your own questions to encourage them to affirm themselves and each other in positive ways.

Discussion Questions:
— How does it feel to talk about yourself to others this way?
— Why is it good to say nice things about ourselves?
— Why is it good to encourage others to acknowledge themselves in positive ways?
— Why is it important to be able to acknowledge ourselves for the things we're good at?
— Who will tell us something you learned about someone else that you didn't know before?

No Time to Be Modest

Art Activity

Materials:

Poster paper and magic markers in various colors.

Directions:

Explain to the children that positive self-talk consists of encouraging words that we say to ourselves that help us succeed. (Remind them of the things they shared in the Sharing Circle, I Succeeded Because I Encouraged Myself. Encouraging words are helpful and powerful, particularly when we put them into positive statements about ourselves. They are especially helpful when we are feeling discouraged, or have some negative feelings about being able to accomplish something.

Explain: *Think of three strong, positive statements about yourself, such as "I am a good athlete," "I am very smart," or "I am a great listener." Your statements should be about things that you want to become skillful at—rather than things you are already skillful at.*

Pass out the materials, and have the children write their statements in large letters on the poster paper. Tell them to use the magic markers to make their statements colorful and decorative. Prepare a statement yourself to show as an example. Tell the children to take their statements home and place them on a wall, or in another location where they will see them often. Tell them that each time they look at their statements, they will become more and more like them.

Discussion: While they work, talk to the children about encouraging words, and how they can help us become more positive and capable. Assist any children who get stuck, or inadvertently include something negative in their statements.

Reinforce the children for the positive statements they make. Point out that although sometimes we're told it's impolite or conceited to say good things about ourselves, these encouraging statements are not like that. They are to help us do things we want to do.

It's OK to Like Yourself

Presentation and Group discussion

Materials:

None.

Directions:

Introduce the activity by gathering the children together and telling them that you want to discuss a very important matter with them. Explain: *I want to tell you about three children who are your age. As you listen to these descriptions, see if you can tell whether or not these children like themselves.*

In your own words present the following three character sketches*:

Brian: The first thing people notice about Brian is his friendliness. He likes talking to everybody in his class and to adults, too. When you talk to Brian, he listens. He frequently jokes and plays around in enjoyable ways. Brian thinks people are fun and almost everybody likes him a lot. Brian usually has a smile, but at times he becomes sad, angry, or scared of something. He isn't the smartest boy in his class but he learns well. He isn't the best looking either.

Carrie: The first thing people notice about Carrie is that she doesn't have much to say to most people. She acts as if her classmates aren't as good as she is. She does like two other girls in her class, and so she talks to them. She also likes her teacher. She talks to her, but not to most other adults. Carrie rarely shows how she is feeling. She hardly ever laughs and almost always seems bored. She is very smart and very pretty.

Joe: *The first thing people notice about Joe is that he is a good looking boy. Then they notice that he usually doesn't speak in a normal voice. He shouts. He shouts orders and put-downs at other children. Joe acts as though he would fight anyone who did anything to bother him. It's easy to tell how Joe is feeling, and most of the time he seems to feel like he's in charge. Like Brian, Joe is not the best student in the class, but when he pays attention and tries, her does will with all of his subjects.*

Encourage the children to discuss the characters by asking:
— Which of these children do you think really likes himself or herself?
— How can you tell?
— How does someone like Carrie who acts superior to others probably feel about herself deep inside?
— How does someone like Joe who acts as if he has the right to boss other people around probably feel about himself?
— Why do people like Brian so much? Does it help the he likes himself?

After the children respond, suggest this point of view: *Brian really likes himself. Because he likes himself, he is able to like other people and treat them well. Carrie and Joe probably act superior and bossy because they don't like themselves very much and are trying their best to hide it. One of the reasons Brian is attractive to others is the he likes himself.*

Add the following key point: Sometimes people don't realize that it's okay to like themselves. It's not only okay, it's a necessary part of being fully happy and getting along well with others.

* Change the names of the characters, if necessary. Avoid using the names of children whom your students know.

Dear Me...

Letter-Writing Activity

Materials:

Writing paper and pens or pencils. One envelope and one first-class postage stamp per child.

Note: For maximum impact, do this activity after the children have completed the Experience Sheet, Mirror, Mirror—What to Say to Yourself.

Directions:

Tell the children that they are going to write a very special letter to themselves. They are to be exceedingly complimentary, and include all the encouraging words they can think of. The letter should contain only positive comments and remarks—nothing negative or discouraging. It should recognize their good traits, attributes, and accomplishments, and should inspire them to keep working on areas in which they want to improve. Set the tone by sharing several sample sentences with the children.

Pass out the materials. Tell the children to begin writing. When they are finished, have them address and stamp their envelopes. Collect the letters, and put them away in a safe place for three months. Then mail them to the students.

Discussion: While the children are busy writing, circulate and offer assistance. Remind the children of how important their words are, and how they are affected by them. Point out that since television, the internet, and people seem to bombard us with negatives, at times, we need all the positive input we can get.

Mirror, Mirror — What to Say to Yourself

Experience Sheet

Sometimes other people say discouraging words to us. And sometimes, we say discouraging words to ourselves, too. When we listen to discouraging words, we begin to have doubts about ourselves. That's when we need help.

Try this:

On a separate piece of paper, write down 3 of the most negative things you've ever said to yourself—or that someone else has said to you.

Now rewrite those negative statements, so that they are positive and encouraging.

Example: I'm just no good at math.
Change to: Math problems are easy and fun to solve.

1. _____
2. _____
3. _____

Now try this:

Take the paper with the discouraging words on it, and shred it into bits. As you throw the bits of paper away, tell yourself that you are throwing away all those discouraging thoughts and beliefs. They are gone.

And this:

Sit in front of a mirror and repeat your positive statements aloud to yourself several times. Say them with great strength and feeling. Look yourself squarely in the eye as you speak. Convince yourself that these things are true!

Making Positive Choices

We are the products of the choices we make. When we learn this, and become conscious of our choicemaking, and of the consequences of our choices, we can direct our lives onto positive and productive paths The first step toward making wise choices is making positive ones! This unit provides children with experiences that allow them to become conscientious, productive choicemakers.

Something I Chose That Made Me Happy

A Sharing Circle

Directions:

Introduce the topic: *Our topic for this session is, "Something I ChoseThat Made Me Happy."*

Elaborate: *Think of a time when you had a choice to make. Maybe you had to choose something you wanted to do, or what clothes you wanted to wear, or a place you wanted to go. The choice could have involved something really special, or just something ordinary, but whatever it was, you were pleased with the results of your choice. Take a moment and think about it. The topic is, "Something I Chose that Made Me Happy."*

Invite the children to take turns sharing. Listen carefully to each one and, through your example, assist the other children to do the same. Don't allow negative interruptions. Be sure to take a turn yourself.

Discussion Questions:

When everyone in the circle has had a chance to speak, ask the children:
— How many different kinds of choices do we make every day?
— What are some choices that might have made you unhappy in the situation you shared?
— Does thinking about being happy help us make good choices?

A Hard Choice That I Had to Make

A Sharing Circle

Directions:

Introduce the topic: *Our topic for this session is, "A Hard Choice That I Had to Make."*

Elaborate: *Can you think of a choice that you didn't want to make, but had to make anyway? Maybe the choice involved something you had to tell someone, or an unpleasant job you had to do. Or perhaps you were going to put off doing something, but decided to go ahead and do it after all. Take some time and think about it. The topic is, "A Hard Choice That I Had to Make."*

Invite the children to take turns sharing. Listen to each one carefully and help the other children do the same. Don't allow negative interruptions. Be sure to take a turn yourself.

Discussion Questions:

After everyone in the circle has had a chance to share, ask the children:
— How did you feel when you remembered the hard choice that you made?
— Are there times when choosing isn't as hard as we think it will be? Why do you think that is?

What Do You Really, Really, Really Want

Art/Creative Thought

Materials:

Enough colored notebook-size paper so that each child has three sheets. White glue, scissors, pens or pencils, and plenty of magazines that children look at or read.

Directions:

Place the materials on large tables and divide them evenly among the children. The children will be cutting words and pictures from the magazines and gluing them to their sheets of colored paper. They can also create drawings and designs to supplement what they find in the magazines.

Explain: *We are going to make pictures of the things we really, really, really want to have in our lives. Take a moment and think about what you would like most to have, to be, to see, or to do. Now, make a list of the three most important things you want. Cut out pictures and words that describe what you want from the magazines, and glue them to your paper. You have one sheet on which to show each thing you want. If you like, make drawings and designs of your own. As the children work, watch to see if you can assist anyone who is having difficulty. Let them be as creative as they wish. There is no right or wrong way to do this activity; however, the wants that the children depict need to be positive. Allow enough time for work and cleanup.*

Discussion: During the activity, assist where you can, and reassure the children that they are doing fine. Ask the children to talk about their choices, acknowledging each child with appreciation.

Extension:

Conduct a sharing session during which the children each display one of their sheets and talk about what they've chosen and why.

We Decided to Do It This Way

Group Choice and Presentation

Materials:

One hundred pennies, beans or some other item that can represent money for each group. Writing paper, and pens or pencils.

Directions:

Have the children form groups of four or six depending on the total number of children involved. Each group will receive one hundred pennies (or beans), which will become that group's treasury. Together the children will cooperate to make choices about how best to use this treasury.

Explain: *Each group has been given one-hundred pennies (or beans). Pretend that each penny (or bean is a dollar, so that you really have one hundred dollars. Working individually, I want you to think of the very best way to use your group's money. Then, when we're all ready, you'll work with the others in your group to make one choice from among all of your ideas about how to use the money. When your group has made its choice, write it down.*

Allow time for individual thought, and offer any help needed for the children to make their individual decisions. After several minutes, ask the groups to start making their group choices. Ask each group to indicate when it has completed the task. Don't proceed until all groups are finished. During the activity you may want to offer some suggestions. When the groups have finished, ask each to present its choice. Be sure to acknowledge each group's efforts.

Discussion Questions:

After all the groups have shared their choices, ask the children the following questions:
— Was it easy or difficult for you to make a choice on how you would spend the money for yourself?
— Was it easy or difficult for your group to make a joint decision on how to spend the money? What was the difference?
— What are some things that people can do when they have to make a group decision that will make the process easier for them?
— What did you learn from this activity about getting along with others.

Choose in the News

News Review and Discussion

Materials:

Current newspapers (one for every two children), scissors, writing paper, and pens or pencils.

Directions:

Organize the children into pairs, and give a newspaper and other materials to each pair. The children will be reviewing headlines and articles that show choices that people make, and the results or outcomes of those choices. They will cut out the articles they choose, and write down both the choice and the outcome described in each article.

Explain: *Work with your partner to find two articles in the newspaper. Look at the headlines. Pick one article in which a person, a group of people, or an organization made a choice that caused something good to happen. After that, find an article that describes a choice that caused something bad to happen. Cut out the articles, and write down the choice and outcome for each one.* As the children work, pass among them and give help, where needed.

Discussion Questions:

After all pairs have finished, ask the group, *What is the difference between a choice and an outcome, or result?* Now ask the children to share their articles and the choices and outcomes they recorded. After the presentations, ask the group the following questions:
— In the articles with bad outcomes, what other choices could have been made?
— If another choice had been made, what might have been the outcome?

Extension:

Have the children write short newspaper articles about choices they have made, and the outcomes of their choices.

Choices I Made Today

Log Keeping and Discussion

Materials:

A Copy of the experience sheet, "If I Get To Choose . . . and I Do!" for each child.

Directions:

Hand out the Experience Sheets and introduce this activity to the children by saying: You may not think of it this way, but you are always making choices. With the help of your Experience Sheet you're going to look at the choices you make every day. Use your Experience Sheet to write a list of all the choices you make during a day.

For the next twenty-four hours, everytime you make a choice, write it down. After each choice, write the outcome. Sometimes outcomes happen right away, like choosing something to eat and having it taste good. Sometimes outcomes don't happen for awhile. For example, when you save money to buy something, the outcome doesn't happen until enough money is saved to buy the thing you want. See how many choices and outcomes you can write down in a day. Tomorrow, we'll talk about all the choices we made.

At the end of the day, remind the children to complete their lists and to be sure to bring them back to the next day's class.

Discussion Questions:

At the next meeting, have the children share some of the choices and outcomes they recorded. After all of the children who wish to have shared, spend time discussing their experiences. Ask them:
— Did you make some choices without thinking?
— What were some big choices you made?
— What were some little choices you made?
— Do you think you wrote down all of the choices you made?
— What were some choices you made that had immediate outcomes?
— What were some choices whose outcomes won't happen for awhile?
— Were you surprised at how many choices you made?

If I Get to Choose . . . and I Do!

Experience Sheet

For one entire day keep track of all the choices you make. Write about what each choice was and what the outcome was, or will probably be.

1. **A choice I made:** _____

   What happened because of the choice I made: _____

2. **A choice I made:** _____

   What happened because of the choice I made: _____

3. **A choice I made:** _____

   What happened because of the choice I made: _____

4. **A choice I made:** _____

   What happened because of the choice I made: _____

5. **A choice I made:** _____

   What happened because of the choice I made: _____

Communicating Effectively

Some of the most important skills we can learn are those that relate to effective communication. Individuals who consistently speak and listen accurately have greater control over themselves, and greater influence in dealing with others. This unit is designed to help the children focus on the speaking, listening, and body language aspects of communication, and to identify ways in which they can improve their abilities in all areas. Additionally, the activitoies help the children develop a keener awareness of how important it is to communicate well.

Someone I Like to Talk With

A Sharing Circle

Directions:

Introduce the topic: *Our topic for this Sharing Circle is, "Someone I Like to Talk With."*

Elaborate: *Being able to talk with other people is very important for all of us. Most of us find that certain people we know are easier to talk with than others. Can you think of someone with whom you enjoy having conversations? Perhaps the person you like to talk with is a good friend your own age, or a teenager—or maybe he or she is an adult. Tell us about the person and what kind of conversations you have. Let's take a few silent moments to think it over. The topic is, "Someone I Like to Talk With." Invite the children to take turns speaking. Model good listening by showing the children what a good listener you are. Don't allow negative interruptions. Be sure to take a turn yourself.*

Discussion Questions:

After each child who wants to speak has done so, ask the children:
— Why are conversations with the people we talked about so satisfying?
— Do all of these people have similar qualities and abilities and, if so, what are they?"
— Is being able to speak well an important ability for each of us to develop? Why?

A Time I Listened Well to Someone

A Sharing Circle

Directions:

Introduce the topic: *The topic for this session is, "A Time I Listened Well to Someone."*

Elaborate: *We've been doing a lot of talking and sharing in our Sharing Circles, and we have also been listening well to each other. If we hadn't been good listeners, our circles wouldn't have worked. Listening is just as important in communication as talking. Can you think of a time when you listened carefully to another person? Perhaps you had a friend who needed to talk about a problem and you showed you cared by listening and saying very little. Or maybe it was a situation in which you learned a lot from someone who had some interesting and important things to say. Think about times like these, when you used your listening skills, and tell us about one of them. Let's take a few moments of silence to think it over. The topic is, "A Time I Listened Well to Someone."*

Invite the children to take turns speaking. Listen carefully to each one and guide the other children to do the same. Don't allow negative interruptions. Be sure to take a turn yourself.

Discussion Questions:

After each child who wants to speak has done so, ask the children:
— Can you tell if someone is listening to you or not?
— When you know someone is listening, how does it make you feel?
— How do you feel when the person you are talking to isn't listening?

Correct Cues Can Be Crucial

Practice in Precise Communication

You Will Need:

An outdoor or indoor area with numerous large objects, such as plants, furniture, trash cans, etc.

Directions:

Set up an obstacle course using the plants, furniture, trash cans, etc. This will be the "runway" over which the "pilots" in this activity must be guided. Talk with the children about how important it is for people to communicate clearly and accurately. Ask them to imagine what would happen if airplane pilots didn't communicate clearly with air traffic controllers, or quarterbacks didn't communicate accurately with their football teams. Airplanes would crash, and football teams wouldn't be able to run their plays.

Blindfold one child and spin him or her around at one end of the runway. This person is the pilot. Station a second child at the other side of the runway— the pilot's destination. Announce that this person is the air traffic controller.

Explain: When you are the air traffic controller, it is your job to guide the pilot (called "Captain") step-by-step through the obstacles using words only. If the pilot touches anything, it counts as a crash, and your turn is over. The pilot may direct questions to the air traffic controller. The rest of us will be very quiet during the exercise.

Give everyone a chance to try both roles.

Discussion Questions:

After everyone has had a turn, ask the children:
— What can we learn from this experiment?
— How can misunderstandings happen when we don't communicate clearly?
— What are some examples of other situations in which it would be essential to communicate very clearly?

Extension:

Ask a pilot, air traffic controller, or high school quarterback to visit the group. Encourage the children to ask questions about how the guest communicates precisely with others on the job. Urge the visitor to give a few examples of precise communication.

The Big Muddy

Group Experiment and Discussion

Directions:

Ask the children to sit down with you in a circle. Then explain: *This may seem like a Sharing Circle, but it's not. This is an experiment called, "The Big Muddy." I'm going to whisper something into the ear of the person on my right, and try not to let the rest of you hear what I say. Then he or she will whisper it into the ear of the person on her right, and he or she will do the same, until everyone has heard the message and whispered it to the next person. After the last person has heard the message, he or she will say it out loud. Then I will tell you what I said in the beginning. Let's do it and see what happens.*

Begin the experiment: As the message is whispered, encourage the children to be as quiet as possible, and to observe each whisperer and listener in turn. Ask the last person who hears the message to repeat it out loud. Then tell the group what you said to the first person when you started the experiment. The difference between the two messages will probably cause amazement and laughter.

Ask the children why they think the activity is called, "The Big Muddy." After they respond, suggest that they do the activity again, and ask a volunteer to start a new message. As time allows, give as many children as possible an opportunity to start a message.

Discussion Questions:

Between messages, talk with the children about how communication can become muddy when it is passed from one person to another many times. When the activity is complete ask the following questions:
— Why do you think the first message is so different from the last message?
— How can poor communication cause misunderstandings between people or groups?
— What kind of similarities did you notice between what happened in the activity and gossip or rumors?
— What did you learn from this activity?

Clear Directions Are Important

A Game of Communication

Materials

Blindfold, pins, either a pin-the-tail on the donkey game that you bring in or use the template provided of pin-the-ball on the seal's nose game

Directions

Talk with the children about the importance of communicating clearly and accurately. Tell them that they are going to practice giving clear directions and listening carefully by playing the familiar game, "Pin the Tail on the Donkey" (or "Pin the Ball on the Seal's Nose").

Post the target of the donkey (or seal) in an area clear of desks, chairs, and other obstacles.

Ask the children to form pairs. Explain that the partners must work together in order to win the game. One partner must give very clear, accurate instructions, and the other must follow them very carefully to try to pin the tail on the donkey (or the ball on the seal's nose).

Have the first pair come forward. Blindfold one child and spin him or her around a few feet from the target. Then step aside and have the child's partner guide the child to the target using only words. Make certain that the tail (or ball) is pinned securely to the donkey (or seal) before removing the blindfold. Repeat the procedure with the remaining pairs. Award a prize to the pair whose tail (or ball) is closest to the correct spot on the target. Have the partners switch roles and play the game again.

Conclude the activity with a discussion.

Discussion Questions

— What was hard about giving directions?
— What was difficult about following directions?
— When you were blindfolded, how confident were you that your partner would not let you get into trouble?
— Why is it so important to communicate clearly in this game? ...to listen carefully?
— What are some examples of other situations in which it would be important to communicate very clearly and to listen carefully?

Record the Message and Play It Back

Dyads and Discussion

Directions:

Talk with the children about how communication involves two functions: 1) giving, and 2) receiving messages. We give messages by speaking, and we receive them by listening. In order to be effective communicators, we have to perform both functions well.

Explain: *Let's see how good we are at receiving messages. I have an activity in mind that will give us a chance to see how well we can listen. The activity is called, 'Record the Message and Play It Back.' You will try to 'record' in your mind what someone says, and then tell that person what you heard, to see if you got it right.*

Ask the children to form dyads, and have them decide who is A and who is B. Then direct them through this process:

First minute: A speaks. Topic: What I Like About My Favorite Game

Second minute: B "plays back" what he or she heard A say.

Third minute: A compliments B and/or makes corrections.

Fourth minute: B speaks. Same topic, or a new one you choose.

Fifth minute: A "plays back" what he or she heard B say.

Sixth minute: B compliments A and/or makes corrections.

If the children would like to repeat the activity, ask them to change partners. Then guide them through the same process, creating your own topics.

Discussion Questions:

Ask the children:
— How did you feel when you listened like a voice recorder?
— How did you feel when you were the speaker, and were listened to so well?
— How did you know you were listened to?
— What did you do that helped you be a good listener?

Other Things To Try:

Suggest that the children try listening very carefully to other people, letting them know they are being heard by repeating back to them some of the things they say. Suggest that they use lead-ins like this: *I believe I really heard you, Mom. You said that ...*

Let Me Understand You

Practicing Communication Skills

Materials

List of situations provided.

Directions

Begin by talking with the children about how much we depend on our ability to communicate with one another. Mention that communication is one of those things that can be very good or very bad. Bad communication leads to misunderstandings. It can cause people to get directions wrong, make mistakes, and feel hurt or angry. Good communication helps people to understand each other and to cooperate and get along. Good relationships develop out of good communication.

On the board, write the following guidelines of good communication. Go over them and talk about why each is important if people want to get along and understand each other.
1. Look at the other person.
2. Listen carefully.
3. Speak clearly.
4. Think about what you want to say.
5. Say what you mean.

Have the children form groups of three to five. Describe one of the situations on the next page to each group, and explain that you want them to act it out using good communication. Give the groups 10 to 15 minutes to plan and rehearse their skits. Then have one group at a time perform its skit for the entire group. Circulate and provide assistance during the planning period by helping the children identify and understand the good communication skills they can demonstrate in their skits. Use these and your own questions to facilitate discussion after each skit is performed.

Discussion Questions

— Did the actors look at each other while they were communicating?
— How well did they listen?
— Could they have expressed themselves more clearly? How?
— What else could they have said?
— What happened as a result of this communication?
— What have you learned about good communication?

Situations

- You are looking for a missing book and think that a group of children might have it or know where it is.
- Someone asks to play on your team, but you already have enough kids.
- You and your friends must decide what each person will bring to a picnic.
- You don't understand what the teacher has asked you to do.
- You want to meet and make friends with a new student.
- You want to eat lunch with kids you usually don't eat with.
- All the kids around you are whispering and making noise, so you can't hear what the teacher is saying.

Communicating with My Body and Face

A Feelings-Pantomine Game

Materials

Index cards, marking pen, and a small box to hold the index cards

Directions

Using the "Feeling Words" list provided, or a list of your own, print one feeling word on each index card. Place the index cards into a box.

Either one at a time or in pairs, have the children reach into the box and draw one feeling-word card. Caution them not to tell the rest of the class which card they selected. After all of the children (or pairs) have a card, direct them to take a few minutes to create a pantomime demonstrating their feeling word. Explain that they are to act out the word with their bodies and faces; they may not say words or make noises. Circulate and provide assistance and encouragement.

Have the children perform their pantomimes for the rest of the class. After the class has shown its appreciation with applause, ask the children to guess the feeling that was demonstrated in each pantomime. If they have difficulty, have the performing group provide hints.

Facilitate discussion between performances.

Discussion Questions
— How can you tell when someone is angry at you?
— What kinds of facial expressions show joy? Fear? Doubt?
— How does feeling sad affect the way you sit and walk?
— What does it mean to "read" someone's feelings?
— Who understands your feelings better than anyone? How do they do it?

Feeling Words

happy	naughty	friendly
jealous	proud	beautiful
warm	lazy	angry
brave	guilty	left out
scared	confused	comfortable
loving	lonely	sad
homesick	sick	peaceful
nervous	afraid	ignored
shy	relaxed	tired
powerful	stupid	sleepy
silly	worried	grumpy
excited	hungry	embarrassed

Speak Up, Speak Clearly!

Skits and Discussion

Materials:

Copies of Communication Scenarios (one copy per group). A copy of the Experience Sheet, "Can you Say It Better?" for each child.

Directions:

Begin by talking with the children in a general way about how much people depend on their ability to communicate with each other. Mention how communication is one of those things that can be very good or very bad. Bad communication causes misunderstandings and other problems. Bad communication can result from unclear communication, or no communication at all. Give examples of unclear or noncommunication, and ask the children how each could create misunderstandings. Ask for examples from the children as well. As a way to help the children to start thinking, distribute the Experience Sheets, and tell the children that you'd like them to fill in the speech bubbles of the cartoon characters on their own. Read the descriptions of the two situations, and allow some time for the children to fill in the blanks on their sheets.

After they have filled in their Experience Sheets, have the children form small groups. Tell them that they are now going to act out some situations involving communication.

Explain: I'd like each group to plan and rehearse two short skits. In the first skit, act out the situation the way it is written, showing how poor communication caused problems. In the second skit, using the same basic scenarios, have the characters communicate better, so that no problems occur. Each skit should be 1 - 3 minutes long. Depending on the total number of children, different groups may act out the same skit. Give the children time to plan and rehearse their skits. Then ask them to perform for the total group.

Discussion Questions:

At the end of each small group's second skit, ask the children:
— Do any of these situations remind you of times when you were involved in a misunderstanding? What happened?
— Why is it important to communicate clearly and completely?
— What can you do to better understand someone who doesn't communicate completely or clearly?
— What can you do to make sure you communicate well?

Communication Scenarios

Unclear Communication:
- Your friend has an argument with his big sister and comes to school in a bad mood. When you see him, he doesn't want to talk and says he wants to eat lunch alone when you invite him to join you. You wonder if you did something to make him upset with you.
- Your parent calls you "an exceptional child" in front of company. You don't know just what your parent means or whether to be pleased or embarrassed by the comment.

No Communication:
- You and your friends plan a party. Everyone says that he or she will bring something either to eat or to drink. You all show up with things to eat, but nobody brings anything to drink. You each blame the others for not planning better.
- You have an argument with a friend and decide to write a note saying you are sorry. Your friend gets the note but doesn't respond. You don't know if your friend is still upset or accepts your apology.

Can You Say It Better

Experience Sheet

Here are two situations in which kids are not communicating well. Read each one. Then follow the directions—and help them communicate better!

Situation 1: Randy and Sue like each other, but both are a little shy. Sue just got a new haircut, and Randy thinks it's cute. When she looks at him, he says, "Hey, your hair is short and it's too neat!" He sticks his fingers in her hair and messes it up. The other kids laugh. Sue moves away quickly. She thinks to herself, "I guess Randy doesn't like my new haircut, and he doesn't seem to like me anymore either."

What could Randy say instead? What could Sue say to him? Fill in the bubbles.

Situation 2: Bill and Bud are pals. They decide to go on a five mile hike to the top of a big hill. They agree to meet at the one mile point. Bill says, "It's going to be great! I'll bring some stuff." Bud says, "Yeah, that's good. So will I." They meet at the right place at the right time, but each boy has a blanket and a snake bite kit. Neither has food or water, and they are already hungry and thirsty.

What could Bill and Bud say to each other to make a better plan? Fill in the bubbles.

Being Responsible

We all have responsibilities, and are accountable for our behaviors at home and work alike. Children need to develop responsible behavior patterns in order to take charge of their own lives. They need to learn that being accountable means taking credit—and blame—for their actions. The activities in this unit will help children become aware of ways in which they are (or can become) responsible. In addition, the children will explore and rehearse ways to demonstrate their trustworthiness.

A Way in Which I'm Responsible

A Sharing Circle

Directions:

Introduce the topic: *The topic for today's Sharing Circle is, "A Way in Which I'm Responsible."*

Elaborate: *Think of a responsibility that you accept and carry out. It may be a chore that you do each week, like sweeping the kitchen floor or watering the lawn. Perhaps your responsibility is to do your homework every evening after dinner, or to read a half hour each night before bed. Maybe you get up on time every morning, or fix breakfast for yourself and your younger brothers or sisters. Do you earn and save money? That is a way of being responsible. Before we begin, think quietly for a few moments about something you do that is responsible. The topic is, "A Way in Which I'm Responsible."*

Give each child an opportunity to speak. Listen carefully and encourage the other children to listen too. Thank each one for sharing, and remember to take a turn yourself.

Discussion Questions:

After the sharing in the circle is completed, ask the children:
— Do we all have a way in which we are responsible?
— What did you learn by listening to what other children do that is responsible?
— Why do you think it is important to have responsibilities?

I Admitted That I Did It

A Sharing Circle

Directions:

Introduce the topic: *The topic for our circle today is, "I Admitted That I Did It."*

Elaborate: *Can you think of a time that you did something—either good or bad—and then admitted that you did it? Maybe it was something accidental, like breaking a glass at a friend's house. Or perhaps it was something that you were ashamed of, like taking money from your mom's purse. Maybe it was something that you were proud of, but a little shy about admitting. For example, you might have baked fancy cookies for a class party at school, but felt too embarrassed to tell anyone that you made them. Whatever it was that you did, you took responsibility for it and admitted that you did it—even though it might have taken a lot of courage. Let's think about it quietly for a minute before we share. The topic is, "I Admitted That I Did It."*

Let the children take turns speaking. Encourage them to listen carefully while each child speaks. Thank each child for his or her contribution, and don't forget to share yourself.

Discussion Questions:

After each child who wants to speak has done so, ask some key questions:
— Why is it sometimes difficult to take responsibility for the things we do—whether bad or good?
— Why do you think it is important to take responsibility for what we do?

Trust Walk

Activity and Discussion

You Will Need:

A large room or outdoor area that offers a variety of shapes, textures, and objects for the children to explore, by touch. Blindfolds, such as scarves, dish towels, or pieces of cloth.

Directions:

Explain to the children that this is an activity in which partners work together to build trust. Tell them: *One partner will be blindfolded and the other will bet he guide. When you are the guide, lead your "blind" partner around the room or outdoor area safely and carefully, while providing opportunities for him or her to touch different objects, listen to sounds, and smell various aromas. Don't talk during the activity. At the end of 10 minutes, I'll give a signal and you will change places with your partner. After 10 more minutes, I will signal you to return to the group to share what happened on your Trust Walk.*

Have the children choose partners. Tell them to decide who will be the guide and who will be the blindfolded person during the first round. Stress the responsibility of the guides to provide a lot of experiences for their partners— but in safe ways. Also remind the children that they may not talk during the exercise. Suggest that they agree on *how* the guide will lead the partner; for example, by holding hands or by linking arms. They may establish *nonverbal* signals to indicate left, right, up, down, fast, or slow.

Discussion Questions:

After each partner has had a turn to be both a blindfolded person and a guide, gather the children together for a discussion and debrief of their experiences. Ask them these questions:
— What were some of the things you experienced on your walk?
— How did you feel being the guide?
— How did you feel being guided?
— What was it like to do the activity in silence?
— What did you learn about being responsible?

Be Eggs-tra Careful!

Activity and Discussion

Materials:

Raw eggs (one per child), and colored magic markers.

Directions:

Tell the children that they are going to have the responsibility of taking care of something very fragile and delicate for one whole day. They will be given a raw egg to take with them everywhere they go for the next twenty-four hours. Give each child a raw egg. Tell the children to decorate the eggs with magic markers, making sure not to break them. Have them name their eggs, and treat them like special friends. If you like, break an egg on a plate or in a bowl, to help the children see how "heartbroken" an egg becomes when it is not properly cared for.

Say to the children: *You must take your raw egg with you everywhere you go for the next twenty-four hours. You may set it on the table while you eat or put it on the nightstand while you sleep, but you may not hide it. It is your responsibility to protect your egg from harm and keep it company. Bring it back next time we meet, to show that you kept it safe.*

Discussion Questions:

The next time you meet, lead a discussion of the experiences the children had protecting their eggs. Ask them:
— What did you do to protect your egg during your daily activities?
— What did you say to other people about your egg?
— Did you have any "close calls," or did you let your egg get broken?
— How did you feel about being in charge of something so fragile for a whole day?
— What did you learn about being responsible while doing this activity?

Critter Talk

Creative Role Play

Materials:

Whiteboard, or butcher paper and magic markers.

Directions:

In this activity, the children will assume the role of their pet, in order to understand the animal's perspective. Begin by brainstorming the kinds of pets that the children have or would like to have. List them on the board or butcher paper. Then discuss the care that each animal would require in order to stay healthy and happy. Be sure to include exercise, shelter, food and water, companionship, affection, pest control, and cleanliness. This will bring to awareness the needs of each kind of animal, so that the children can more easily role play their chosen animal.

Ask the children to think about their own pet—or the pet they would like to have. Say to them: *Now that we have listed various kinds of pets, and the care each needs to survive and be happy, put yourself in the place of that animal and think about what it would say about you if it could talk. What would your pet turtle, Horace, say about how you care for him? Would your dog, Fluffy, say that you take her for a run every morning and evening? Do you think your guinea pig, Grover, would brag about how clean you keep his cage? Pretend you are your pet and talk with a partner who is taking the role of his or her pet.*

Ask volunteers to come before the group, two or three at a time, to role play their pets in an animal "chit chat." Encourage them to say what their animals would really say if they could talk. Suggest that they assume the mannerisms of the animals, but focus on how their owner or master takes care of them. Allow 1 1/2 to 2 minutes per scenario.

Discussion Questions:

After the role play, ask the children:
— In what ways did you become more aware of the needs of your animal when you took its role?
— What would happen to your pet if you were not responsible in caring for it?
— How is having a pet a big responsibility?

What Time Is It

Discussion and Art/Writing Activity

Materials

A real or toy clock with moveable hands or a paper-plate clock (directions provided); drawing materials

Directions

Ask for a show of hands from the children who wear a watch or know someone who wears a watch. Ask them why people wear watches, and why most rooms in offices and homes have clocks. Through discussion, make these points:
- Watches, clocks, and digital time displays tell us the time of day.
- We need to know the time of day because we use the 24-hour "clock" to organize our lives. We go to school at certain times, eat at certain times, sleep at certain times, etc.
- Other people depend on us to be on time for our activities and appointments.

Talk to the children about the importance of being on time. Ask them to talk about times when they were late, what happened, and how people who were waiting felt or how they felt when they had to wait for someone who was late.

Use a clock with moveable hands (or make a clock with the directions provided) as a visual aid during the class discussion. Place the hands of the clock to show different times that things happen each day, such as when school begins, lunch time, and when after-school begins. Ask the children to show the time they go to bed, the time of their favorite TV show, and the time they get up in the morning.

After the discussion, have the children draw a picture or write a story about a real or imaginary incident in which they were late. When they finish, have them share their pictures or stories with the rest of the group.

Discussion Questions

— What would happen if every member of a soccer team showed up for practice at a different time?
— What would happen if the school bus driver arrived at the kids' bus stops at a different time each day?
— Why is it important to be on time for appointments?
— How does showing up on time demonstrate that you're a responsible person?
— If a friend is waiting for you, why is it important to be on time?

Directions for Making a Paper-Plate Clock

Materials – paper plate, paper fastener, marking pen, and 1 sheet of heavy construction paper

Write the hours with a marking pen around the outside edge of the paper plate. Cut out big and little hands from construction paper. Attach one end of each hand to the center of the paper plate with a single fastener. Make sure that the holes in the hands are large enough to enable the hands to rotate around the fastener.

One of My Responsibilities

Art Activity

Materials:

Newsprint or art paper, pencils, black construction paper, white glue, colored chalk, facial tissues, and hair spray.

Directions:

This activity can be used right after the Sharing Circle topic, A Way in Which I Am Responsible.

Place the materials on a table or workspace. Tell the children that they are going to draw one of their responsibilities with glue on black paper. After the glue dries, they will fill in the spaces with colored chalk.

Explain: *Think of one of the ways in which you are responsible and draw it with pencil on the newsprint. It may be something you shared in the Sharing Circle, or some other responsibility. For example, you might want to draw your hand holding a dog's water dish under a faucet—or yourself getting up on time in the morning. Experiment by drawing a variety of sketches. Keep your objects big and simple. When you are satisfied with a sketch, draw it on the black paper. Use the white glue to go over the pencil lines.*

Collect the drawings. Let the glue dry for several hours or overnight; it will be transparent when dry. Tell the children to fill in the shapes with colored chalk, using only one finger to spread the chalk evenly. They can clean their finger with a tissue as they change chalk colors, and wash their hands when they are done. Seal the pictures with a light coating of hair spray to keep the chalk from smearing.

Discussion: As the children work, talk about those responsibilities that they consider the most important. Ask them how they feel about what their pictures depict. Display the completed pictures around the room before sending them home with the children.

An Interview With a Parent

Experience Sheet

Take this sheet home and interview your parent or guardian about his or her responsibilities. Then bring it back and share your findings with the rest of the group.

Person being interviewed: _____

Interviewer: _____

What is an important responsibility that you have at work (or home)?
Answer: _____
_____

What do you think are your most difficult responsibilities as a parent?
Answer: _____
_____

In what ways are you rewarded for being responsible?
Answer: _____
_____

Do you have any responsibilities that are fun? What are they?
Answer: _____
_____

What responsibilities did you have when you were my age?
Answer: _____
_____

How can I be more responsible at home?
Answer: _____
_____

Following Rules

Every place we go has rules and standards we are expected to follow. Generally, these rules help protect us from harm. For example, speed limits keep us safer on the road. Other rules help maintain order and protect our rights and the rights of others. Knowing how and why such rules exist usually makes children more willing to follow them. This unit will help children understand what rules are, and how they make systems, games, and our lives function better.

A School Rule I Appreciate

A Sharing Circle

Directions:

Introduce the topic: *Our topic for today is, "A School Rule I Appreciate."*

Elaborate: *Sometimes we take rules for granted. We don't stop to think what would happen if we didn't have rules to guide our behavior. Think about all the different kinds of rules you have at your school, and tell us one that you appreciate. It can be a classroom rule, or a playground rule, or a rule that is for the school in general. In deciding, consider the ways you benefit from the different rules. Perhaps you're happy there is a "no hitting" rule because you are small. Or maybe you appreciate a "taking-turns" rule because you are shy and wouldn't get a turn without such a rule. Think about it for a few moments. The topic is, "A School Rule I Appreciate."*

Invite the children to take turns speaking. Listen carefully to each one and encourage the other children to do the same. Allow no negative interruptions. Make sure you share too.

Discussion Questions:

After everyone who wants to speak has done so, ask the children:
— What rules were mentioned most often?
— Why do you think they were mentioned more than others?
— How do rules make things go more smoothly?
— What do you think would happen if there were no rules?

Something I Did to Improve Our Environment

A Sharing Circle

Directions

Introduce the topic: *Our topic for this session is, "Something I Did to Improve Our Environment."*

Elaborate: *Think of a time when you did something to improve your surroundings. It could have been picking up trash in your yard or on the school grounds, or painting over graffiti on a wall. It could have been planting a tree, pulling weeds, taking out the trash, or painting a mural on a blank wall. Improving the environment can involve either cleaning up an area, or making an area more beautiful by adding something to it. Take a few moments to think of a time when you made an improvement in one of these ways. The topic is, "Something I Did to Improve Our Environment."*

Invite the children to share. Listen carefully and encourage the other children to do the same. Thank each child who shares. Remember to take a turn yourself.

Discussion Questions:

After everyone who wants to speak has done so, ask the children:
— Which is more fun, cleaning up an area, or adding something to beautify it? Why?
— What do you think would happen if we didn't do things to keep our environment clean?
— What are some areas you know of that could be made more attractive?

Why Do We Have Rules

Discussion and Art Activity

Materials

Construction paper or poster board; colored marking pens, paints, or crayons

Directions

Begin by asking the children to think of rules they are expected to obey at school, at after-school, at home, and in the community. Call on volunteers to state various rules while you write them on the board. Examples of possible rules are:

School
- Do not leave class without permission.
- No talking during tests.
- Listen to the teacher.
- No cutting in line.

After-school
- Don't leave until an authorized adult comes to pick you up.
- No running in the halls
- No hitting or pushing.
- Share toys and books.

Home
- No TV or video games until homework is done.
- Pick up and put away toys you are not using.
- Don't leave the property without parent permission.
- Do your chores without being told.

Community
- No skateboarding on city sidewalks and streets.
- Cross streets at corners and within crosswalks.
- Obey traffic signals.
- No littering.

When you have a lengthy list of rules, take a look at each one. Ask the children:
- Why do we have this rule?
- Who or what is the rule designed to protect?
- What would happen if we didn't have this rule?
- Is this a necessary rule, or an unnecessary rule?

Facilitate discussion, encouraging the children to actually think about the rules instead of merely accepting and obeying, or resenting and ignoring them without question.

As a follow-up to the discussion, have the children each choose a rule that they consider important and create a poster depicting that rule. Suggest that they print the rule in large letters and draw a picture of a child or adult obeying or disobeying the rule. When finished, allow each child to hold up his or her poster and tell the group why they chose that role. Display the posters around the room.

Discussion Questions
— Who makes the rules in your home? ...at our school?
— Who makes the rules in our city?
— What would our class be like if we all did exactly as we pleased?
— If you could make a new rule for school or home, what would it be?

If I Ruled the World...

Fantasy/Group Activity

Materials:

A box containing cards or slips of paper, each with a different rule written on it. (Examples are: "Trash must not be thrown out of car windows." "People may not possess illegal drugs.") Paper and pens.

Directions:

Introduce the activity by asking the children: *Why do we have rules or laws? Are they really necessary?*

Have a volunteer pull a card and read the rule on it. Ask, *What's one possible reason for this rule? or Why would someone have made this rule?* Lead a discussion about the importance of rules.

Have the children form groups of three or four. Tell them that each group is going to create an imaginary land, and establish a set of rules for the people who live there.

Explain: *Give your land a name, agree on what it is like, and decide who can live there. Then establish a set of rules, and decide what will happen to people who don't cooperate with those rules.*

Discussion: As the children are creating their lands, encourage them to look at the "whys" of their rules, and at what would happen if they didn't have such rules.

Ask volunteers to describe their lands and the rules they established for people who live there. Take advantage of this time to discuss and reinforce specific rules that are necessary to maintaining order.

Other Things To Try:

In preparation for the initial discussion, instead of writing rules on cards yourself, have each of the children think of a rule and write it down.

Rules and Rhymes

Poetry/Art Activity

Materials:

Paper, crayons, magic markers, and Shel Silverstein's book, Where the Sidewalk Ends.

Directions:

Distribute the materials. Tell the children that each of them is going to have an opportunity to write a poem about one or more rules, and draw a cartoon to illustrate the poem. Read Shel Silverstein's poem, "Sarah Cynthia Sylvia Stout Would Not Take the Garbage Out," and show the children the illustration that accompanies it. Show them other pages in the book too, so they can see several examples of the simple line cartoons that illustrate the poems. (As an alternative, written and audio versions of this poem are available on the internet.) Next, ask the children to think about rules that they would like to make, change, or get rid of. Generate enough discussion to help each child decide on a subject for his or her poem. Tell the children to start the writing/illustrating process.

Discussion: As the children work, talk with them about the rules they picked to be the subjects of their poems. Encourage them to keep their poetry light and humorous. Praise the children for their ideas, rather than for the quality of their writing or art work.

When they are finished, have the children share their poems. Then collect the cartoons and compile a cartoon book.

Extension:

Have the children make a book of poems and cartoons based on the lands they created in the *If I Ruled the World* activity.

It's All in the Game

Game Creation and Discussion

Materials:

Two boxes, and various objects to place in the boxes (like whistles, balls, sticks, marbles, buttons, tools, etc.), paper, and pens.

Directions:

Introduce the activity by asking the children to think of some games they like to play. Pick two or three of the games they mention, and discuss the rules that govern them. Divide the children into two groups, Give each group a piece of paper and pen, and a box with some objects in it.

Explain: *Look at the objects in your box. Your task is to create a game with those objects. Decide what rules are necessary in order for the game to work. Are there any penalties for breaking the rules? If so, what are they? Give the game a name, and write the rules on the sheet of paper. Each group will then teach the other group how to play its game, explaining the rules that govern it.*

During the activity, be encouraging. Offer some suggestions if the children really get stuck, but allow them as much independence as possible.

Have each group take a turn teaching its game and rules. Play each game for a short period of time.

Discussion Questions:

After playing both games, talk about each of them. Ask:
— Would any other rules help make this game more fun?
— Were any of the rules unnecessary?
— Should any of the rules be changed?
— Why is it important for people to follow rules?
— What would happen to the game if the players didn't follow the rules? . . . Would the same thing happen in real life if people didn't follow rules?

Rules Are Rules

Experience Sheet

Think of the many different areas of your life in which you are required to follow the rules. Then answer these questions:

The best rule at home or school is: _____

_____

The worst rule at home or school is: _____

_____

It should be changed because: _____

_____

If I were in charge of the world, here are three rules I would make immediately:

Rule: _____

Reason for rule: _____

_____

Rule: _____

Reason for rule: _____

_____

Rule: _____

Reason for rule: _____

_____

Understanding Body Language

Even the most convincing of words isn't as true an indicator of how someone feels as is that person's body language. Even in silence, body language speaks loudly and eloquently—but it also has the effect of underscoring spoken language. Clearly, words convey only a part of each message. We can tell a great deal about other people by their expressions, gestures, and movements, and those same indicators reveal to others a great deal about us. This unit is designed to help children become more aware of the unspoken messages that they exchange with others on a daily basis.

Someone Didn't Say A Word, But I Knew How He or She Felt

A Sharing Circle

Directions:

Introduce the topic: *Our topic for today is, "Someone Didn't Say A Word, But I Knew How He Or She Felt."*

Elaborate: *We tend to think we communicate with just the words we speak. However, we also give off clear messages without saying a word. Or we say words, but our bodies say something very different from our words. Think of a time when someone you know didn't say a word, yet you took one look and knew that person was unhappy or angry or delighted or scared. Describe how you think the person felt, and what it was about how the person looked that communicated his or her feelings so clearly. Take a few moments to think it over. The topic is, "Someone Didn't Say A Word, But I Knew How He Or She Felt."*

Invite the children to take turns speaking. Listen carefully and encourage the other members of the circle to do the same. Thank each child, and remember to take a turn yourself.

Discussion Questions:

After everyone who wants to speak has done so, ask the children:
— How were you able to tell what the person was feeling without being told?
— What were the most obvious clues to the person's feelings?
— If you didn't know someone, do you think you could tell how that person was feeling? Why or why not?

I Didn't Say a Word, But They Knew How I Felt

A Sharing Circle

Directions:

Introduce the topic: *Our topic for today is, "I Didn't Say a Word, But They Knew How I Felt."*

Elaborate: *In the last circle, we talked about being able to determine the feelings of others without their telling us. In this circle, think of a time when another person, or a group of people, knew how you were feeling, even though you didn't tell them. Maybe you were disappointed, joyful, embarrassed, confused, angry, or thrilled. Whatever the feeling was, someone could see it in you, and told you so. Take a few minutes to think of such a time. The topic is, "I Didn't Say a Word, But They Knew How I Felt."*

Invite the children to take turns speaking. Listen intently and thank each child who shares. Don't allow any negative interruptions. Be sure to take a turn yourself.

Discussion Questions:

After everyone who wants to speak has done so, ask the children:
— Was it OK, or were you uncomfortable knowing that others could tell how you were feeling?
— How do you think the others knew what you were feeling?
— What was good about someone's being able to figure out how you felt?

That's a Fine "How-Do-Ya-Do"

Verbal/Nonverbal Experiment and Discussion

You Will Need:

An unobstructed, open space; and a watch or clock for timing.

Directions:

Explain: *Mill around the room and greet as many people as you can in five minutes. Try to use different words and methods to greet each person. It's OK to say something someone else has said, but you must not use the same greeting twice.*

Tell the children to begin. Call time at the end of five minutes.

Explain: *Mill around and greet everyone again, but this time do it nonverbally. You may use gestures, movements, facial expressions, even sounds, but **you may not use words!** Again, it is OK to do something that someone else has done, but don't use the same method twice. Greet everyone in the group differently.* Tell the children to begin, and call time at the end of five minutes.

Discussion Questions:

At the end of the experiment, call the children together and ask:
— How did you feel when you couldn't use words?
— What are some nonverbal greetings you used that you had never thought of before?
— What similarities did your greetings have?
— Which method did you think was most effective—verbal or nonverbal?
— Even when no words we're used, could you tell what the other person was communicating to you?

Let Your Feelings Be Your Guide!

Movement/ Observation Activity

Materials:

A list of situations, each of which generates a different emotion or reaction. For example, "Your teacher just caught you looking on someone else's test paper;" "Your mom just said you can have a puppy;" "You just lost your homework;" "You are home alone and you hear strange noises outside your bedroom window;" "Your little sister or brother has been fooling around in your room;" "You have just been given a good citizenship award from the school principal."

Directions:

Ask the children to form a circle. Have them extend their arms outward and touch each other's outstretched hands. This will allow plenty of space for movement.

Explain: *When I call out a situation, you must respond nonverbally in a way that seems appropriate to that situation. For example, if I say, "You have just won the lottery," you might do this: (Demonstrate by jumping up and down, waving your arms, or letting your mouth drop open). Now show me how **you** would respond to the lottery example. While you are reacting, notice the reactions of others too.*

Encourage the children to really "get into it."

Call out another situation such as, "Your best friend just moved to another city." Allow enough time for the children to respond. Remind them to respond nonverbally, and to look around and make mental note of the different ways in which the other children respond.

Continue calling out situations until you have exhausted your list.

Discussion Questions:

Generate a discussion by asking these and other questions:
— What kinds of actions or gestures were used for positive reactions? For negative reactions?
— Can you recall seeing someone react differently than you did to the same situation?
— What did you notice about people's facial expressions?
— What have you learned about communication from this activity?
— Do you always need words to communicate what you're feeling, or to understand what someone else is feeling? . . . Explain.

Other Things To Try:

Have the children create and call out situations, or simply **feelings** that can be expressed nonverbally.

Take It From the Back

Role Play and Observation

Materials:

Three boxes or other containers. In the first box, place approximately 15 slips of paper on which you have written the names of emotions or moods, such as mad, sad, furious, irate, happy, etc. (It's OK to repeat emotions, but include as many different ones as you can.) In the second box, place approximately 10 slips of paper on which you have written body parts, such as arms, shoulders, feet, and head. (These too can be repeated.) In the third box, place about 5 slips of paper on which you have written different roles, such as teacher, parent, coach, or bus driver.

Directions:

Gather the children together and tell them: *Today you are going to have a chance to do some role playing, but you are not going to use any words. You will use only your body to get the message across. And when it's your turn to take part in a role play, you'll do it with your back to the rest of us. We will try to guess what emotion you are acting out.*

Choose two or three volunteers for the first role play. Have them silently draw one slip from the emotion box, turn their backs to the group, and independently (and nonverbally) act out the emotion they've drawn. Ask the group to guess what emotion is being dramatized. Ask for new volunteers and do two or three more rounds like this one.

Next, have the players draw both an emotion and a body part. This time when they turn their backs to the group, they must act out the emotion using only that one body part. Do three or four rounds in this manner, with the large group guessing the emotion.

Finally, have the players draw both an emotion and a role; for example, "mad" and "grandmother." Repeat the procedure described above.

Discussion Questions:

Following the activity, generate a discussion by asking these and other questions:
— Were you surprised that you could correctly identify emotions from the back? . . . from the movement of only one body part?
— Which emotions or moods were the toughest to determine?
— What were some of the main indicators of anger? fear? sadness? etc.

Checkin' It Out

Observation and Discussion

Materials:

The Experience Sheet entitled Take a Close Look! (one per child).

Directions:

Gather the children together and tell them: *We've done several activities in which we've role played different feelings and situations, observed each other's nonverbal behavior, and tried to figure out what emotions were being expressed. Now we're going to practice our observation skills where we can observe people we don't know expressing **real** feelings.*

Pass out the Experience Sheet *Take a Close Look!* and ask the students to quietly observe others and to write about what they see on their experience sheets. Remind them that you will discuss what they have observed at the next class meeting.

Discussion Questions:

At the next class session, lead a discussion regarding the children's experiences. Ask them:
— What kinds of feelings did you observe most often?
— Which moods/feelings were easiest to identify?
— Are you more aware of body language now than you used to be?
— Was it easier to write what you observed, or to draw it?

Take a Close Look!
Experience Sheet

If you look closely, you can tell how people feel by the **expressions on their faces**, and by the **way they move their bodies**.

Go to a busy place where you can sit down and watch lots of people go by. **Look closely, and write down what you see.**

Describe a happy person:

head _____

eyes _____

mouth _____

shoulders/arms _____

hands _____

posture _____

legs/feet _____

Draw a picture here:

Describe an angry person:

head _____

eyes _____

mouth _____

shoulders/arms _____

hands _____

posture _____

legs/feet _____

Draw a picture here:

Describe a tired person:

head _____

eyes _____

mouth _____

shoulders/arms _____

hands _____

posture _____

legs/feet _____

Draw a picture here:

Describe a sad person:

head _____

eyes _____

mouth _____

shoulders/arms _____

hands _____

posture _____

legs/feet _____

Draw a picture here:

Making and Keeping Friends

Cooperation, support, and having fun together are some of the things we experience with our friends. Our network of friends is one of the most important areas in which we develop social awareness. Children learn skills for interacting with others through successful interaction with their peer group. And having friends to care for and rely on can help them cope effectively with life's daily challenges. This unit is designed to help children develop the ability to establish and maintain friendships. The children will explore the responsibilities of being a friend, and learn what behaviors might cause them to lose friends. In addition, they will have the opportunity to experience directly some of the benefits of friendship.

Something I Like About One of My Best Friends

A Sharing Circle

Directions:

Introduce the topic: *The topic for our circle today is, "Something I Like About One of My Best Friends."*

Elaborate: *Most of us have several close friends, or "best" friends. Think about one of the things that you especially like about one of your best friends. Is it how he treats you? Could it be that she walks home from school with you everyday? Perhaps your friend is funny, or helps you with your spelling. Maybe he plays two square with you at recess. Don't tell us your friend's name, just the special thing that you like about him or her. Let's take a minute to think quietly about it before we share. The topic is, "Something I Like About One of My Best Friends."*

Invite each child to take a turn speaking, while everyone else listens carefully. Be sure to take a turn yourself.

Discussion Questions:

After the sharing, ask the children:
— Were we able to think of one thing that we liked about a friend?
— How were these things alike or different?
— Why is it important to think about what we like in a friend?

Something I Do to Keep a Friend

A Sharing Circle

Directions:

Introduce the topic: *Our topic for today's session is, "Something I Do to Keep a Friend."*

Elaborate: *We all have new friends and old friends. What is it that we do to keep a friend for a long time? Think about one of the things you do to make certain that someone will keep choosing you as his or her friend. Are you kind to him? Do you play ball with her after school? Do you invite him to ride his bike with you to the park on Saturdays? Maybe you help him or her practice the multiplication tables. Perhaps you share your ice cream with her when you buy one. Think quietly about it for a few moments before we start. The topic is, "Something I Do to Keep a Friend."*

Invite the children to take turns speaking, and encourage them to listen to each other carefully. Be sure to take a turn yourself.

Discussion Questions:

After each child has had a chance to speak, ask the children:
— Were we all able to think of something that we do to keep a friend?
— How were these things alike and different?
— Why is it helpful for us to think of something that we do to keep a friend?

Friends Support Each Other

A Cooperative Game

You Will Need:

An outdoor space, free of glass, rocks, or holes; or an indoor space with mats or carpeting.

Directions:

Brainstorm with the children ways in which friends give each other support. Include suggestions such as, "encouraging friends to do their best in a ball game or race," "helping friends with chores or homework," and "sharing P.E. equipment." Also include "listening to friends when they have important things to say," "sharing feelings," and "consoling friends when they are upset." Discuss with the children how they feel when supported by *their* friends in these ways.

Tell the children that they are going to play a game in which they give each other physical support. It is a fun game in which friends may end up struggling, stumbling, and giggling, as well as supporting each other. They will start with one partner, and add another each time they accomplish their task. Say to them: *You will begin the game by sitting on the ground, back-to-back with your partner, knees bent and elbows linked. All you have to do is stand up together. With a little practice and cooperation, it will be pretty easy.*

After the partners have mastered standing up back-to-back, have some of them divide and join other partners to make groups of three, with the same task. Then try groups of four, five, and so on. A whole group stand-up can be achieved by having everyone sit close and stand up quickly, at exactly the same moment.

Expect a lot of giggling and falling over. Don't be concerned if the large group stand-up doesn't work. The fun is in the trying.

Discussion Questions:

After groups of various numbers have made several attempts to stand up, gather the children together and talk about how they felt when they were able to stand up together. Ask them:
— How did it feel to support each other, and cooperate with one another?
— Was it easy to do every time?
— What made it difficult? Easy?
— Did you have to think about the other kids in your group to make it work?

String Painting With a Partner

Art Activity

Materials:

White construction paper, one 2-foot piece of string per child, and tempera paint in several colors.

Directions:

Tell the children that each of them, along with a partner, is going to participate in a cooperative art activity. Partners can make two paintings so that each child can take home one of them. Before the activity begins, have the children pair up. If there is an extra person, you can be his/her partner.

Place the materials on large workspaces. Have each pair decide on two colors for its string painting. Contrasting colors, such as red and blue, or a light and dark color, work best. Tell the children: *First, fold your drawing paper in half. Then reopen it. One of you will dip your string into a color of paint, holding onto one end of the string. Carefully place the painted string on one half of the paper, creating some kind of a design. Keep holding the dry end of the string, and let it stick out of the paper, while your partner folds the other half of the paper over the string. Your partner will then press lightly with his or her hands on the outside of the paper while you pull out the string. Open the paper. Next, your partner will repeat the process with his or her string, using another color of paint, and will make a design over yours while you press on the paper.*

The result will be a beautiful two-color butterfly, with one color underneath the other. Let each team make two paintings. Be sure to allow time for clean up.

Discussion: As the children work, ask them how they feel about creating a piece of art as a team. *Do they need to have some special talent to do this? Do they need to cooperate to accomplish the task? Is it fun?* Have the partners share their paintings with the group.

Other Things To Try:

See if the partners would like to "dance" their paintings. Have them notice how the two colors relate to each other on the paper. What shapes and directions do they take? Play some music and let the partners choreograph their string paintings.

How to Make and Keep A Friend

Roleplay and Discussion

Directions

Lead a discussion on friendship by saying in your own words to the children:

"We all want to be treated in friendly ways. One of the best ways to be treated well ourselves is to be a good friend to others and treat them well. So let's talk about friendship today. Let's act out, and show one another, how friendship really works. To get started, let's make a list of some ways to make friends- ways that work well. Then we'll make a list of ways to keep a friend.

Write the heading, "Making Friends" on the board and list the strategies that the children describe. Do the same under the heading "Keeping Friends". Add any additional strategies that you think are important.

Next, tell the children that you have some ideas for situations they can act out using the strategies on the list. Have the children form groups of three or four. Assign one of the situations listed on the next page to each group and tell them to plan and perform a role-play of that situation. Give half the groups a situation from the "Making Friends" list and the other half from the "Keeping Friends" list.

Give the groups time to plan and rehearse their role-plays. Circulate and observe the rehearsals. Assist with planning as necessary. Make sure all the children have a role to play when they act out their situations.

When the children have finished rehearsing, have each group take a turn acting out its situation. Use the Discussions Question to facilitate a discussion after each performance.

Discussion Questions:
— Why is it helpful for us to think of something that we do to keep friends? To make friends?
— What are some behaviors that cause people to loose friends?
— What have you learned that can help you keep friends? ...make a friend?

Situations for the "Making Friends" Role-Plays
1. You are playing a game with some of your friends in your front yard. A new girl in the neighborhood walks up and stands nearby watching.
2. The teacher asks you and a boy in your class whom you don't know very well to take a box of books to the library. You believe this boy is much smarter than you are.
3. A family of a different race moves into a house on your street. The family includes two children about your age. One day the children come out of the house just as you walk by on your way to school.

Situations for the "Keeping Friends" Role-Plays
1. Your friend calls you, but you just sat down to dinner with your family and it isn't a good time to talk.
2. Your friend had a fight with her big sister and is feeling terrible.
3. You are at the movies with a friend. Just before it starts, another friend comes over and sits beside you and says, "Hi." These two friends of yours don't know each other.

A Basket Full of Friendship

Craft Activity and Discussion

Materials

Colored construction paper for making flowers; green construction paper for making stems and leaves of different sizes; brown construction paper for making baskets; pencils, scissors, glue, and marking pens

Directions

Write the heading "friendly" on the board. Ask the children what the word means. Talk about its definition. Ask the children to think of words that describe and encourage friendliness between people. List the words that they suggest on the board. For example:

- sharing
- smiling
- warm
- caring
- outgoing
- agreeable
- easygoing
- happy

Next, write the heading "understanding" on the board. Follow the same procedure, listing characteristics such as:

- kind
- thoughtful
- forgiving
- considerate
- patient
- giving

Tell the children that they are going to create baskets filled with paper flowers that represent some of the characteristics of friendly and understanding people.

Distribute the colored construction paper, marking pens, scissors and glue. Have the children draw flower shapes on the colored paper and then cut out the fowers. Help your children as necessary with the shapes and cutting. Next, instruct the children to choose one word from either list and write it in the center of a flower. Tell them to write a different word on each flower.

Distribute the green construction paper, pencils, and scissors. Show the children how to draw stems and leaves of different sizes, cut them out, and glue them to the flowers. Circulate and assist as the children work.

Distribute the brown construction paper and show the children how to cut out a basket shape. Show the children how to glue their flowers to the back of the basket. Circulate and assist them to complete their baskets of flowers. Display the flowers on tables and desks around the room.

Use these and your own questions to stimulate discussion about friendly and understanding behavior

Discussion Questions
— How do you know when someone is friendly?
— How can you tell when a person is understanding?
— Is it possible to be friendly with everyone?
— When is it important to be understanding?

The Power of Praise

Acknowledging Each Other in Writing

Materials:

Small squares of writing paper, pencils, paper lunch bags, crayons or colored markers.

Directions:

Begin this activity by asking the children how they feel when another person compliments them or acknowledges them for doing something well. Ask volunteers to share their feelings. Explain that all people need and want to hear positive things about themselves. Hearing praise from others makes people want to keep doing the things for which other people are praising them. Tell the children that they can encourage and support each other by exchanging positive words of praise on a regular basis.

Tell the children that they are going to have an opportunity to practice giving each other positive acknowledgments so that this behavior can become a positive habit.

Give each child a paper lunch bag and some crayons or colored markers. Ask each child to print his or her name on the bag in large letters and decorate the bag with crayons or markers. Suggest that the students draw designs, symbols, or pictures that represent something about themselves.

When the bags are decorated, give each student a stack of writing paper equivalent in amount to the number of students in the class.

Give the following instructions:

Pass your bag to the person on your right (in front, in back, etc.). When you receive a bag, look at the name on the bag, take the first piece of paper from your stack, and write a note of praise to that person. The note should contain some positive words about the person or his or her accomplishments. No put downs or criticisms are allowed. You do not have to sign your name to the note. When you are finished writing the note, put it in the bag and pass it to the next person; keep passing the bags until you receive your own bag back, full of positive notes.

Make sure each child gets a positive statement from each other child.

Set aside time for the children to read the notes they receive. Invite the children to share their most meaningful notes of praise and tell why those notes are especially positive, encouraging, and/or supportive. Ask the children to share how they feel about receiving acknowledgments from their peers. Conclude by discussing the importance of verbally acknowledging others and sharing feelings of appreciation. Ask the following questions and any others of your own.

Discussion Questions:
— Why is it important for us to acknowledge each other with positive words?
— How would our lives be different if we supported each other daily with words of praise and acknowledgment?
— What must you do in order to have something positive to say to each person in class? . . . to your friends? . . . or in your family?

Let Me In

Game and Discussion

Directions

Locate a large, open space where the children can move about freely and make noise.

Number the children off randomly to form groups of seven or eight. Say to them that they will be given a task to perform as a group. One person will stand outside each group and try to break in, while the other children form a tight circle to try keep the person out. The person outside the circle must try his or her best to get inside the circle and the group must try equally hard to keep that person out.

Tell the children that they are not to make it easier for friends. Everyone is given 2 minutes to try whatever they think will work (talking, climbing, etc.) to get into the circle and every child will have a turn to be on the outside.

When a child succeeds in getting into the circle or when time runs out that person becomes a part of the circle and another child will take his or her turn on the outside.

Expect lots of laughter and shouting. Be prepared for frustration on the part of the person trying to break in. Continue the game until all the children have had an opportunity to be on the outside.

When the game concludes, gather the groups together, and by using the following questions or those of your own, consider what it feels like to be left out and consider the value in making room for everyone.

Discussion Questions

— What did it feel like to be outside the group?
— What did it feel like to be part of the group?
— Did your group cooperate? What was your common purpose?
— As a group member, was it more difficult to keep a friend out than someone you didn't know quite so well?
— How did it feel to succeed at getting in? ...to fail?
— What were some of the ways you used to keep others out of the circle?
— What do we do to keep others out of our activities in real life?
— How has this experience changed your feelings about being included and excluded?
— What are some things you can do to help others be included in your activities?

My Circle of Friends

Experience Sheet

1. Write the names of your friends on the lines provided around this "Circle of Friends."

2. Use magic markers or colored pencils to draw **yourself** on the figure without a face. Add **your** name to that line.

3. Draw a circle around each word that describes a good friend. Then draw a line connecting each circled word with a friend that the word describes. It's OK to connect the same word to more than one friend. You will probably end up with lines criss-crossing each other all over the circle!

IMPORTANT: This sheet is private. Take it home and fill it out. Keep it for yourself, so that you can think about your friends and what their friendship means to you. You don't have to show it to anyone, if you don't want to.

Cooperating With Others

No person can be completely independent within a group, no matter how large or small the group is. Cooperation is necessary for a group to achieve a goal, perform a task—or even continue to exist. And every member of a group is dependent upon other members for support. Knowing how to cooperate with others is a valuable social skill. This unit is designed to help the children learn to understand the dynamics of interdependence by participating in cooperative group endeavors. The children will experience the fun and satisfaction of participating in successful group enterprises, and—perhaps—the disappointment that results when someone in the group lets everyone else down.

A Time I Came Through for the Group

A Sharing Circle

Directions:

Introduce the topic: *The topic for today is, "A Time I Came Through for the Group."*

Elaborate: *We are all members of several groups; for example, families, classes at school, clubs, and perhaps baseball or soccer teams. Can you think of a time when you did something that really helped one of your groups? Maybe you helped your class win an attendance banner by coming to school one day when you didn't feel well. Or perhaps you made a good pass that resulted in a goal for your soccer team. Did you ever run to the store for milk or something else that your family needed for dinner? Perhaps you memorized the Cub Scout Promise so that your den could win a prize for having learned it first. Think quietly about it for a few moments before we begin to share. The topic is, "A Time I Came Through for the Group."*

Give each child an opportunity to speak. Listen carefully and encourage the other children to listen too. Thank each child for sharing, and remember to take a turn yourself.

Discussion Questions:

After the sharing in the circle is completed, ask the children:
— How did you feel about coming through for a group?
— How do you think the other members of the group felt?
— Why do you think it is important for everyone in a group to pull together and cooperate?

A Time Someone Ruined It for Everyone

A Sharing Circle

Directions:

Introduce the topic: *Today the topic for our circle session is, "A Time Someone Ruined It for Everyone."*

Elaborate: *Have you ever been with a group when someone did something to ruin the experience for everyone else? Maybe someone in your class shouted out when you were lining up for recess, and the whole class had to stay inside for an extra five minutes. Perhaps someone ruined a birthday party by starting a fight over the biggest piece of cake. Have you ever been to a family outing at which someone started crying or throwing a tantrum, so you all had to go home? Don't mention any names, but tell what the person did to spoil the event for everyone else. Let's quietly give it some thought for a minute. The topic is, "A Time Someone Ruined It for Everyone."*

Let the children take turns speaking. Encourage them to listen carefully while each child speaks. Thank each child for his or her contribution, and don't forget to share yourself.

Discussion Questions:

When the circle session is finished, summarize by asking:
— How did you feel when someone ruined it for everyone else?
— Why is it important to remember that one person's behavior can affect the whole group?

Sponge Painting With My Group

Cooperative Art Activity

Materials:

Large pieces of butcher paper; white construction paper; tempera paints poured into pie tins; sponges cut in half, or quartered.

Directions:

Tell the children that they are going to create an imaginary machine with gears, wheels, and other machine parts. They will work cooperatively in groups to complete the project, but each person's contribution will be unique.

Divide the children into groups of six to eight. Give each group a large piece of butcher paper, several colors of paint (with a sponge for each color), and one piece of construction paper per group member. Each person will then tear his or her piece of construction paper into the shape of a machine part such as a wheel, shaft, gear, or belt.

The first person will place his or her paper machine part somewhere on the large piece of butcher paper and sponge paint around the edges by dipping the sponge into one color of paint and dabbing it onto the paper.

The next person will place his or her part near the first part, and sponge paint around it so that the parts are connected by paint. Repeat the process until everyone in the group has connected a part to the machine. Go around the group again until the children decide that their machine is finished.

As the children work, watch to see if any groups are having difficulty with the activity. Emphasize the need for group cooperation—and for acceptance of every person's contribution. After the machines are completed, have each group work cooperatively to decide on a name, and describe the function of the machine. Then have each group present its machine to the others. Hang up the machines for all to see and enjoy.

Discussion Questions:

When the groups have finished working on their sponge paintings, ask the following questions:
— Was it easy or difficult to work together as a group? . . . Why?
— How did it feel to work as part of a group?
— What did you learn from this activity about working cooperatively?
— What are things you can do to help your group work well together?

Teams of Two

Chair Volleyball Game

Materials

Round balloons (one for each pair of children, plus extras), moveable chairs

Directions

Ask the children to form pairs. Have the pairs spread out around the room. Make sure that each pair has a chair and plenty of space in which to move around. Distribute the balloons. Help the children blow up and tie their balloons.

Ask for a show of hands from the children who have played volleyball. Explain that they are going to play volleyball in pairs, using their balloons as balls and the backs of their chairs as nets. One person will be on one side of the chair, and the other person will be on the opposite side. However, they will not be playing against each other. Explain that each pair is a team and must cooperate to keep their ball in the air as long as possible. All of the pairs will play at once and the pair whose balloon stays in the air longest will win.

Announce one last rule: The children must play on their knees.

Have the children get down on their knees on opposite sides of their chairs, with one child ready to "serve" the balloon. Signal the start of the game. Watch all the pairs. When a pair drops or breaks their balloon, call them out of the game. Allow the game to continue until only one pair remains. Proclaim that pair the winners. Have the children change partners, and continue with additional rounds.

Discussion Questions

— What did you and your partner have to do to keep your balloon in the air?
— What was it like to play on your knees?
— Where did you keep your eyes, on the balloon, your partner, or somewhere else?
— What kinds of movements helped and what kinds made things worse?
— What did your partner do that was helpful? ...not helpful?
— What did you notice your partner doing that showed that they were cooperating with you?
— How did you demonstrate cooperation?

Together is Better

Cooperative Activities

Materials:

Depending on the specific project, drawing or writing materials; puzzles; trash/scrap items: string, glue and other fasteners.

Directions:

Have the students form small groups. Have each group of students work on one of the activity ideas listed below. You may want to choose one activity and assign it to all the groups, or allow each group to choose the activity they want to work on.

Activity ideas:
- Produce a drawing that illustrates a feeling such as anger, sadness, confusion, worry, compassion, or joy.
- Write a short poem about a feeling and illustrate it.
- Create a sculpture, collage, or some other product (provide a variety of small trash items, scraps, and recyclables as listed in the materials list).
- Write a short story that demonstrates a group of children collaborating and cooperating on a project.

Require that the groups demonstrate cooperation and inclusion as they work together, giving equal time and participation to every member of the group and not allowing anyone to dominate the process.

Have the groups show and/or display their final products for everyone to see. Facilitate a culminating discussion.

Discussion Questions:
— What was it like to work together on this activity?
— How did you make sure that everyone had an equal chance to participate?
— Did you experience any conflicts? If so, how did you resolve them?
— Did everyone in your group participate equally? Did anyone dominate? Not do their share?
— How did your group demonstrate cooperation and collaboration?

Let's Skin the Snake

Movement Activity

You Will Need:

A large grassy area, free from holes, stones, or glass—or an open space indoors, with mats.

Directions:

Tell the children that they are going to do a movement activity that will utilize the whole group. It is called "Skin the Snake."

Have the children line up, one behind another. You can use up to 25 in a line. Tell them: *Reach between your legs with your left hand, and grab the right hand of the person behind you. The person in front of you will reach back to grab your right hand, so give it to her. This makes a human chain.* **Don't let go**. *Now, the last person in line lies down on his back. The person in front of him backs up, straddles his body, and lies down on her back right behind him. By now, the whole group is waddling backwards. Lie down when you are last. The snake has been skinned when everyone is lying down. When the last child to lie down has touched his or her head to the ground, he or she gets up and starts waddling forward again, pulling the rest of the group up and forward until everyone is in the original chain.*

This activity can be turned into a relay between two large teams. The only rule is that if anyone breaks hands during any part of the process, he or she must stop and reconnect before moving again.

During the activity, talk about the need for everyone to cooperate in order to accomplish the task. Laughing is expected, but jeering is not allowed.

Other Things To Try:

Another cooperative movement activity is the "Circle Sit." Everyone stands in a circle, shoulder-to-shoulder. Then everyone turns to the right, and very gently sits down on the knees of the person behind him or her. This is very impressive when done correctly, and very funny when bungled.

A Letter to Me From Five Important People

Experience Sheet

We all depend upon each other in many ways. You need your friends, family, classmates, teachers, and other important people. They need you, too. Here's a letter that the important people in your life can help write to you.
Write your name on the greeting line. Then ask five people—children and adults—to each finish one of the sentences in the letter. Have them sign their names at the bottom.

Dear _____

I need you for a friend because _____
_____

Something neat that you did for me that I still remember is
_____

We had a good time together when we _____
_____

Something that I especially like about you is _____
_____

Something that I'm really glad I did for you was _____
_____

Your friends, _____
_____
_____
_____
_____

Helping Others

Help comes in many forms and from many sources. Sometimes we want help and don't get it; other times we don't want help and we get it anyway. Volunteering our time and talents not only helps others, it creates rewarding experiences for us, and can be a major source of self-esteem. Through helping others, we learn valuable social skills and the benefits of making positive contributions. The formula is a simple one: When we see we've made a difference, we feel good. This unit is designed to help children learn to recognize when help is needed and wanted, how they can lend a hand to one another, and how they can work cooperatively with others to serve the community.

I Helped Someone Who Needed and Wanted My Help

A Sharing Circle

Directions:

Introduce the topic: *The topic for this session is, "I Helped Someone Who Needed and Wanted My Help."*

Elaborate: *Can you think of a time when you helped someone do something? Perhaps the person you helped was struggling to carry some things and you offered to take part of the load. Maybe you helped someone work on a project or a math problem that he or she didn't understand. Or maybe you helped someone finish a job so that the he or she could go somewhere, and, as a result of your assistance, the person was not only able to do the work faster, but better. Take a few moments to think it over. The topic is, "I Helped Someone Who Needed and Wanted My Help."* Invite the children to take turns speaking. Listen carefully, thank each child, and don't allow negative interruptions. Remember to take a turn yourself.

Discussion Questions:

After every child has had an opportunity to share, ask the children:
— What similarities were there in the things we shared?
— How did you know the person you helped wanted your help?
— How did you feel knowing you helped someone who needed help?

I Got Some Help I Didn't Want

A Sharing Circle

Directions:

Introduce the topic: *Today the topic for our circle is, "I Got Some Help I Didn't Want."*

Elaborate: *Think of a time when you were working on something, and someone came along and started helping you. The problem was, you wanted to do the work by yourself. You didn't want any help. Maybe you were solving a puzzle, completing a school project, or playing a game, and someone tried to tell you how you should do it. You wanted to figure this thing out by yourself, but someone insisted on helping you. Take a moment to think about it before we share. The topic is, "I Got Some Help I Didn't Want."*

Invite everyone to share. You might want to provide an example by sharing first this time. Thank each child for sharing.

Discussion Questions:

When every child in the circle has had a chance to share, ask the children:
— How did you feel when someone helped, even though you didn't want any help?
— Do you think the other people knew their help wasn't wanted?
— What could you have said or done to change the situation?

The Incredible Human Helping Machine

Creative Movement and Problem Solving

Directions:

Divide the children into groups of four or five. Announce that each group will design an *Incredible Human Helping Machine* to "solve" a particular world problem.

Prepare a list of world problems in advance and post them, or allow the groups to brainstorm their own problems. Examples are: abolishing war, eliminating world hunger, eradicating crime, and curing disease. It's OK if more than one group chooses the same problem.

Explain: *Each member of your group will be a machine part, and all of the parts must work together. Each part must move, make a noise, and have a function in the problem-solving. For example, you might be a part that bobs up and down, making a slurping noise as it gobbles up all the nuclear warheads in the world. You must move around, but you cannot get more than an arm's length away from the other parts that make up your machine. Before you start building, get together and decide what problem you want to solve, how your machine will solve the problem, and how each of you will function within the machine that solves it.*

As soon as the machines are all "up and running," have each group explain and demonstrate its machine to the total group. While the machine is working, walk up and touch one member of the group. Tell the children that the part you touched is now ***malfunctioning***. Direct the other members of the group to try to help that part, while continuing their own functioning. Allow them to assist the malfunctioning part for at least 1 minute. If time allows, cause another part of the machine to malfunction.

Discussion Questions:

Start a culminating discussion using the following questions:
— What did you learn about helping others from this activity?
— What was it like when one part malfunctioned?
— As the malfunctioning part, what was it like when others offered help?
— As members of a 'Cooperate Machine,' how did you feel about one another?

All Part of the Warp and Woof

Art Activity

You Will Need:

Magic markers or crayons in a variety of colors; butcher paper pre-cut into strips approximately 4 inches wide and 6 feet long; glue or paste; tables or other large workspaces; up-beat music to play throughout the activity (optional).

Directions:

Divide the children into two groups— the Warpers and the Woofers. Pass out the materials. Announce to the children that they are going to create a group weaving. Explain that warps are threads or yarns that run lengthwise through a weaving, and that woofs are filling threads that run over and under the warps. Tell them that warp and woof is also an English-language expression that means foundation or base.

Explain: *Draw pictures on your strip of paper that express the **best things about you**. The pictures can tell a story about good things you've accomplished, ways in which you help others, or positive traits that you possess. Have fun. The artistic quality of your drawings is not as important as what they stand for.*

After the children have finished drawing, ask them to show their strips to the group, and explain what their drawings represent. Then move to a large area for the weaving.

Select two 4-inch by 6-foot strips of plain or colored paper to serve as the framing strips for the weaving. Lay them out, six feet apart. Ask one of the Warpers to lay his or her warp between the framing strips, so that the ends of the warp overlap the framing strips. Paste the ends of the warp in place. Keep the work flat. Then have the rest of the Warpers paste their warps parallel to the first warp. Allow a few minutes for the paste to dry.

Have the Woofers weave their strips one at a time, over and under the warps. As the children work, point out that some of the drawings are covered up by the strips (and drawings) of other children. Suggest that this is symbolic of the way we help and support one another. Even though our best qualities aren't always visible, they are there—supporting the qualities of others in the group.

When the weaving is finished, hang it up for all to enjoy.

The Gift I'd Give

Inventing Story Endings and Drawing Pictures

Materials

Drawing materials

Directions

Tell the children that you want them to listen very carefully while you read them the beginning of a story. Explain that the story has no ending, and that the job of each student will be to create an ending for the story and draw a picture of that ending.

Distribute the drawing materials before reading one or both of the following story-starters.

1. A very young boy wants to give his mother a special birthday gift, but he has no money—not a dollar, or a dime, or even a penny. This boy doesn't know anyone who has money, and he isn't old enough to get a job. He is very worried that he won't have a gift for his mother. Then, two days before his mother's birthday, he thinks of something to give her. Draw a picture of the boy and his gift.
2. Two weeks before Christmas, your parents tell you that they don't want you to buy a gift for them. Instead, they want you to do something special for them—something that will please them and make them happy. Draw a picture of yourself doing something for your parents at Christmas.

Have the children take turns showing and explaining their conclusion to the story. Use this sharing process to stimulate discussion about the importance of intention, thoughtfulness, and sentiment in gift-giving.

Discussion Questions

— What were some of the gifts that people gave in their stories?
— What are some other gifts that don't cost any money?
— What is something you can do to make your mother happy without spending a dime? What about your father? What could you do for a friend?
— How difficult was it to think of something to draw?
— What could someone do for you instead of buying you a gift?

Helping Our Community

A Group Service Project

Materials:

Chart paper and magic markers

Directions:

Remind the children of the concept of community service, and talk with them about some of the kinds of things that they, as young people, can do to help others in the community. When you've generated some interest, suggest that the children brainstorm a list of possible projects, select one to do as a group, and develop a detailed plan for completing it.

Facilitate a brainstorming session. Stimulate creative thinking by adding some ideas yourself. For example, *collecting food to help the homeless; doing yard work for a disabled or elderly person; planting trees; writing letters to terminally ill children; stuffing envelopes for some community organization like Hospice; visiting convalescent homes and reading to the patients; cleaning up the trash in a local park; recycling products and donating the money to a worthy cause.* Follow these rules of brainstorming: Record all of the ideas on chart paper; don't allow evaluative comments (either positive or negative) during the brainstorming; keep the momentum going and get as many ideas down as you can.

Help the children narrow down the list by discussing the pros and cons of each suggestion. This is the time to evaluate. When the list has been pared down to just a few possibilities, select a project by consensus, if possible—by majority vote, if not.

Have the children select a project leader. Step aside and let the leader facilitate the planning of the project. From the sidelines, try to ensure that the children set up and follow a workable planning process that includes setting a goal, gathering information (through phone calls, etc.), deciding the specific steps that need to be taken to achieve the goal, appointing individuals to take those steps, and developing an accompanying timeline.

Encourage the children to be solution oriented—to think in terms of how things **can** be done rather than why they **can't** be done. Allow time for additional meetings, as necessary.

Discussion Questions:

When the project has been successfully completed, ask the children:
— What was the most rewarding aspect of the project for you?
— What did you learn from this project that you could use in planning another one?
— What did you learn about working together and helping others?

Extension:

Take photos of the actual project activity, and have the children write reports about their experience. Display the reports and photos around the room. The children can also create a presentation of the project and share it with other classrooms and/or at a parent night.

I'm a Secret Help Pal

Experience Sheet

Choose someone you know, and become his or her "Secret Help Pal" for one week. You'll be like a big brother or sister, and *your pal won't even know it!* **Think of some things you could do for your Secret Help Pal. Here are a few ideas:**

>Include your pal in some of your activities.
>Help your pal with homework or chores.
>Introduce your pal to some of your friends.

Keep a daily log:

I helped _____ in the following ways:

Monday: _____
_____

Tuesday: _____
_____

Wednesday: _____
_____

Thursday: _____
_____

Friday: _____
_____

Saturday: _____
_____

Sunday: _____
_____

What was the best thing that happened when you were helping your Secret Help Pal

_____
_____
_____

Appreciating Differences

Everyone is different. People don't need to change to be like anyone else. We all have special qualities that make us who we are, and those special qualities include such things as language, race, religion, and disabilities. This unit is designed to help children realize that appearance is not as important as the type of person we are—and that it's often what others can't see that counts. Special privileges aren't reserved for certain people. No matter who we are, where we live, or where our families are from, we deserve as much happiness and as many friends as anyone else.

A Way I Show Respect for Others

A Sharing Circle

Directions:

Introduce the topic: *The topic for this Sharing Circle is, "A Way I Show Respect for Others."*

Elaborate: *There are many ways that we can show respect for other people. Tell us about a way that you frequently use. Maybe you remember to say please and thank you, or try never to interrupt others when they're talking, or hold doors when you go through them so they won't swing back and smack the people behind you. Perhaps you try not to say critical things about others, or maybe you listen respectfully to the opinions of people you disagree with. Tell us what you do that is respectful, and how you learned to do it. Think about it for a few moments. The topic is, "A Way I Show Respect for Others."*

Invite each child to take a turn speaking, while everyone else listens carefully, without interrupting. Be sure to take a turn yourself.

Discussion Questions:

After every child who wants to speak has done so, ask the children:
— How do you feel about yourself when you show respect for others?
— If you want to be respected, will showing respect for others help? How?
— Should we show respect for people we don't like? Explain.

A Friend of Mine Who Is Different From Me

A Sharing Circle

Directions:

Introduce the topic: *Today's Sharing Circle topic is, "A Friend of Mine Who Is Different From Me."*

Elaborate: *Think of a friend of yours who is different from you in some important way. Perhaps your friend is of a different race or religion, or is a lot older or younger than you. Maybe your friend would rather read a book while you watch television, or collect aluminum cans while you collect bugs. Do you have a friend who uses a wheelchair, or stutters, or goes to the hospital for dialysis treatments every few days? Don't mention your friend's name, but tell us how he or she is different from you, and what you particularly enjoy about this friendship. Let's think about it for a few moments. The topic is, "A Friend of Mine Who Is Different From Me."*

Invite the children to take turns speaking. Encourage them to listen carefully to each other. Don't allow negative interruptions, and be sure to take a turn yourself.

Discussion Questions:

After each child who wants to speak has done so, ask the children:
— When a person thinks or talks differently, or looks different, does that make him or her less worthy of respect? Why or why not?
— What can we gain by having friends who are different from us?
— What would happen if we insisted that all our friends be just like us?

Walk a Mile in My Moccasins

Experiment, Dyads, and Discussion

Materials:

An extra pair of socks for each child.

Directions:

Have the children form a circle. Explain that they are going to find out what it feels like to walk in someone else's shoes. Tell them to count off by two's. Ask the 2's to remove one shoe and place it in the center of the circle. Tell all of the children to close their eyes. While their eyes are closed, mix up the shoes. Then tell the 1's to reach in and take the first shoe they touch. Tell the children to open their eyes.

Explain: *Find the person whose shoe you have. Put on both of your partner's shoes, while he or she puts on your shoes. If you're not wearing socks, use one of the extra pairs I've provided. If you are wearing socks, but would like to wear an extra pair over your own, that's OK too. Now, take a short walk with your partner and talk about what it's like to wear each other's shoes. If the shoes are too small for you, notice what that feels like, and do the best you can.*

Allow time for the children to walk and talk. Then, still wearing each other's shoes, have the partners sit together and take turns sharing in response to one of the following topics:
- *A Time I Was Misunderstood*
- *I Was Treated Unfairly Because I'm Different*

Tell the children that when it is their turn to listen, they are to be very attentive and do their best to understand their partner's experience.

When their partner is finished speaking, they are to say very firmly and warmly, "I understand." Allow about two minutes of sharing per child.

Discussion Questions:

Have the children form a large group and ask:
— How did you feel when you were wearing your partner's shoes?
— Did you learn anything new about your partner?
— Why is it important to try to understand each other's experiences and differences?

Make Mine a Mixed Bouquet!

Art Activity

Materials:

Colored poster paper, magazines containing photos and illustrations of people and flowers (National Geographic and flower catalogs would be excellent), scissors, glue, and magic markers in various colors. A bouquet containing several different kinds of flowers (optional).

Directions:

Begin this activity by talking to the children about the enormous varieties of flowers that are available to grow, or to buy from the florist. Point out that if they were to go to a florist, they could choose a bouquet made up of only one type of flower, or they could choose a mixed bouquet. Talk about the advantages of choosing a mixed bouquet. Mention that the variety of colors, shapes, textures, and scents would be beautiful, interesting, and stimulating to the senses. (If you brought a bouquet of flowers, use it as an example.)

Compare variety in flowers to variety in people. Point out that the different personalities, colors, backgrounds, religions, and talents in people are even more exciting.

Divide the children into groups of three or four, and distribute the materials. Tell the children that each group is going to make two mixed bouquets—one of flowers, and one of people.

Explain: Look through the magazines, and cut out pictures of different kinds of people, and different kinds of flowers. Find as much variety as you can. On one sheet of poster paper, arrange a collage of the people in the shape of a bouquet. On the other sheet of poster paper, do the same with the flowers, or you may want to make one bouquet using both people and flowers together. When you have finished your arrangements, glue the pictures down. Use the magic markers to draw a vase, and to attach a stem with leaves to each person or flower. Complete the collages by adding additional decorations with the magic markers.

Discussion: Circulate and talk with the children while they are creating. Ask them to guess where the people in their pictures work and live, and how they think the people would get along if they knew they were all part of the same bouquet. Talk about the richness that results from combining many unique individuals—whether they are people or flowers.

When the collages are done, put them up for all to see. Title the display, "Make Mine a Mixed Bouquet!"

This Is My Family

Discussion and Art Activity

Materials

Construction or drawing paper, crayons, or colored marking pens

Directions

Ask the children to indicate the number of people in their immediate family (those living in the home). Talk about the importance of families. Ask volunteers to describe some of the benefits that families provide their members (look after and help support each other, celebrate holidays and birthdays together, offer comfort in times of distress, help in solving problems, etc.).

Have the children list the members of their immediate families on sheets of paper. Ask the children to identify the various family members by name, age and relationship (e.g., brother).

Distribute the drawing materials and explain the assignment: *Draw a picture showing your entire family. Include everyone on your list, plus yourself. After you have finished the drawing, write a short caption beneath each family member's likeness, naming specific ways in which that person contributes to the household. For example, maybe your sister washes the dishes and your mother earns money by working in an office. Who cooks the meals, feeds the pets, does the shopping, and helps with homework? List as many contributions as you can think of for each person. If you run out of room, turn your drawing over and use the other side.*

Circulate and assist any children who have difficulty identifying contributions or writing them down.

Display the drawings around the room. In the next activity, the children will share facts and observations about their drawings.

Discussion Questions

— Which family members were easiest to draw? Which were hardest? Why?
— Why do we live in families?
— How do we benefit by living in families?
— How many responsibilities that you listed are shared by more than one person?
— Why do families need to work cooperatively to get things done?

Families Are Different

Creating a Bar Chart

Materials

The family portraits from the previous activity

Directions

Lead the children in a viewing of the family portraits from the previous activity. As you look at each portrait, have the children count the number of family members. Then compare the size and composition of that family with those viewed previously. Ask the children to name ways in which the families differ. For example, some have one parent while others have two, some include a grandparent or other adult, and the number, gender, and ages of the children vary from family to family. Other differences may include skin color, attire, ethnicity, and the presence or absence of pets.

Ask the children to help you make a bar chart showing some of the main ways in which their families differ. On the board, list the categories horizontally along the bottom. On the vertical axis, list the number of children from zero to the total number in the class. Then as you count the families represented in each category, mark the total on the chart and fill in the bars. Depending on the age and readiness of the children, choose examples that challenge them to consider the benefits of diversity. Possible categories include:
- One parent
- Two parents
- Grandparent
- Other adult
- Children under 5

- Children 5 to 12
- Children 13 to 21
- African American
- Asian
- Hispanic
- White
- Pets

Discussion Questions

— Are all the families the same?
— What new information did you learn about a classmate by looking at his or her family portrait?
— Which family portraits contain something that makes you curious to know more?
— How can we all benefit by learning about the differences in our families?
— How does learning about how we are the same and different help us get along and appreciate each other?

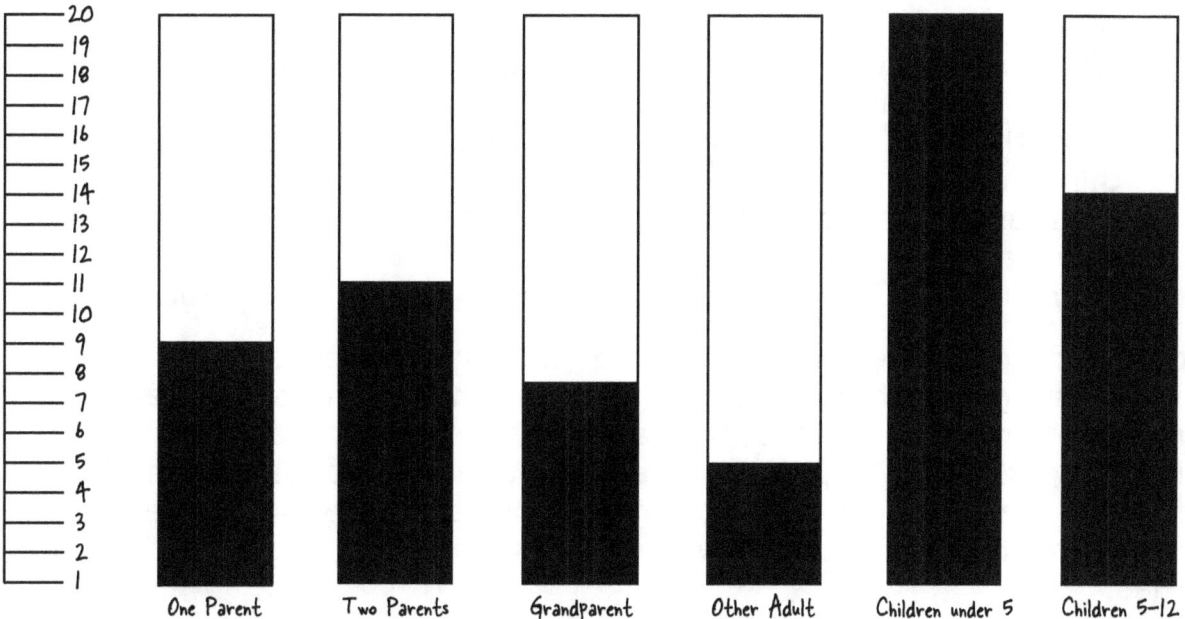

Our Family Backgrounds

Interviews and Discussion

Materials

World, U.S., and regional maps

Directions

Have the children ask their parents and/or grandparents where they were born. Ask them to find out how and why their parents or grandparents came to the U.S. from another country, or to your part of the country from another region.

Give the children a list of questions to ask their parents/grandparents, including:
- What was your purpose in moving?
- What was it like to leave your home and go where you didn't know anyone and had no idea what to expect?
- What things were the same in both countries/regions, and what things were different?
- What are some problems people encounter when they move to a new place?
- How long did it take you to make friends in your new home?

Post the maps where everyone can see them. As the children take turns sharing the information obtained from their families, use flags or other markers to indicate the places on the map where parents/grandparents lived. Help the children gain an understanding of the distances traveled. Talk about the modes of transportation used and emphasize the differences between travel today and travel in earlier times.

Create a chart showing how many countries and states of origin are represented in the class. Include a place on the chart for native children. Make sure that the names of all of the children are included.

Discussion Questions

— What is the most interesting thing you learned from your parents/grandparents that you never knew before?
— How do you stay in touch with relatives who live far away?
— Why is it important to learn about the places our families came from?
— How can we benefit as a class by having people from many different backgrounds?
— Why do you think the United States is known as a melting pot of people?

Celebrating Our Differences

Group Discussion

Materials:

White board or chart paper.

Directions:

Have the children sit in a circle. On the board or chart paper, write these terms: *race, religion, gender, disability, ethnicity, economic level, place of residence, education, values.*

Discuss the meaning of the terms, giving several examples of each. Point out that these are some of the major ways in which people are different. Ask the children:
— How do people react to these differences in others?
— What would the world be like if we were all the same?
— How do you feel when you are with someone who is different from you?
— If you feel uncomfortable around someone who is different from you, what can you do about it?
— How do you feel when someone puts you down because you are different?

Have the children pair up with the person next to them. Tell them to turn toward each other, without leaving the large circle. Say: *Look at your partner. Notice as many things as you can about your partner that are different from you. Tell your partner one of the things you notice. Listen while he or she tells you how you are different. Then think about the ways in which you and your partner are the same, and take turns describing to your partner one of those similarities.*

Discussion Questions:

Facilitate a discussion by asking the following questions:
— What did you notice that was the same about you and your partner? What was different?
— What did you learn about yourself?... about your partner?
— Why do you suppose we spend so much time focussing on our differences rather than our similarities?
— What are some ways in which people and groups benefit from individual differences?

Counting on Each Other

Brainstorm and Discussion

Materials:

One copy of the Experience Sheet *Count On Me!* for each student; whiteboard or chart paper.

Directions:

Ask the children to help you brainstorm some of the many different ways people count on one another in the classroom and elsewhere. List their ideas on the board or chart paper. To facilitate, ask such questions as:
— What do we count on each other for?
— What do you count on me for?
— What do you count on your parents for?
— What do you count on your neighbors for?
— What do you count on your best friend for?

Divide the children into small groups of 8 to 10. Distribute the Experience Sheets. Announce that you want the children to think about the unique qualities, talents and abilities of each person in their group and write down one way in which they count on that person. Tell them to use the list on the board for ideas. Circulate and offer help as needed and make sure what is written is positive. When the children have finished, ask the groups to share, within their small group, what each wrote about the other. When everyone has shared, conclude with a class discussion.

Discussion Questions:

Ask the following questions:
— How do you feel knowing that you can count on so many people?
— How do we learn to rely on other people?
— How do you let others know they can count on you?
— How does knowing you can count on someone build trust?

Count On Me!
Experience Sheet

I can count on _____ to _____
_____.

I can count on _____ to _____
_____.

I can count on _____ to _____
_____.

I can count on _____ to _____
_____.

I can count on _____ to _____
_____.

I can count on _____ to _____
_____.

I can count on _____ to _____
_____.

I can count on _____ to _____
_____.

I can count on _____ to _____
_____.

I can count on _____ to _____
_____.

Managing Anger And Fear

We all experience anger and fear, and most of us have trouble dealing with these feelings at times. People who experience a great deal of trouble with anger and fear sometimes have poor relations with others because of this. This unit is designed to help children better understand these difficult emotions, and to develop positive strategies for handling them. It will also help them distinguish between those fears that are real and those that are imagined, and utilize creativity in deciding how they will respond to feelings of anger and fear.

Something That Really Makes Me Angry

A Sharing Circle

Directions:

Introduce the topic: *Our topic for this session is, "Something That Really Made Me Angry.*

Elaborate: *Think of a time something made you angry—a time that you'd feel OK telling us about. It could be a time when someone treated you unfairly, or a time that you were angry with yourself for breaking or losing something you liked. Or perhaps you were mad because you couldn't do something you wanted to do. It can be anything big or small that made you mad. If it involves another person, dont use their name. Just tell us what happened. Let's take a few quiet moments to think it over. The topic is, "Something That Really Made Me Angry."*

Invite the children to take turns sharing. Listen carefully to each one and encourage the other children to do the same. Don't allow negative interruptions. Be sure to take a turn yourself.

Discussion Questions:

After each child who wants to speak has done so, ask the children:
— How do our bodies react when we are angry?
— What are some things we can do when we are angry to change how we are feeling?

A Time I Was Scared

A Sharing Circle

Directions:

Introduce the topic: *Our topic for this session is, "A Time I Was Scared."*

Elaborate: *Lots of things can be scary to all of us. Think of something that scared you. Perhaps you were at home alone and heard noises, or maybe you were afraid that you wouldn't be included in some activity or event. It might have been that you wanted to do something really well and were afraid you would fail—by striking out when someone was in scoring position, or by letting someone down who was counting on you. Take a few silent moments to think it over, and remember, "A Time I Was Scared."*

Invite the children to take turns speaking. Listen carefully to each one and encourage the other children to do the same. Don't allow negative interruptions. Be sure to take a turn yourself.

Discussion Questions:

After each child who wants to speak has done so, ask the children:
— What similarities and differences did you notice in the fears we shared?
— What are some ways we could lessen our fears or even make them disappear?

I Can See It All Now

Relaxation Activity

Materials:

Optional: relaxing instrumental music.

Directions:

If you have music, play it at a low volume so you can speak over it easily. Make your voice loud enough to be heard, but soft enough to be relaxing. Read the following passage slowly, pausing when you see two dots (. .) so the children have ample time to picture things in their minds as you read.

Explain: *You are going to use your mind to take an imaginary trip. Sit in a comfortable position with your eyes closed so that you can imagine things as I talk to you. Make sure you are not touching your neighbor. Uncross you arms and legs, close your eyes, and take a deep breath. Slowly let it out like this. (Demonstrate this.) Now you do it. Breathe in and let it out. Again. (Continue to breathe in and out with them three to five times.) As you relax . . and take in one more full, deep breath . . and exhale . . excellent . . relax . . Allow your imagination to help you recall a time you were angry. . It may have occurred recently or a long time ago . . a time when you were angry and upset . . Put yourself in that moment . .What do you see? . .What do you hear?. . Can you remember what you said?. . What was it?. . Is there shouting?. . or silence?. . What did you do?. . Did you hit? run?. . break something?. . say things you wish you hadn't?. . Now think of how you wish you had acted . . Could you hit a pillow instead* *of someone? . . or talk to a friend? . . or write your feelings out? . . exercise? . . Picture the perfect way for you to react to this situation . . What can you say? . . What can you do differently than before? . . See yourself saying exactly the right thing at the right time . . Tell yourself, "I have wonderful self-control" . . "I know many positive ways to handle anger" . . good . . And now, as you gradually shift back to the present moment, allow those positive feelings and ideas to stay with you . . You can call upon these skills any time you choose . . Notice that your breathing is becoming stronger as you gently open your eyes, feeling perfect in every way.*

If you're using music, keep it playing. The children may want to stretch.

Discussion Questions:

Ask if anyone would like to share how he or she turned anger into a positive action. Thank those who choose to share. If no one shares, simply tell the children that the imagining technique will work for them anytime and they can use it to help deal with anger situations.

Other things To Try:

A similar relaxation activity can be done using fear as the area to be managed.

Actions Speak Louder Than Words

Brainstorming and Pantomime

Materials:

Chart paper and magic marker or white board, slips of paper, and a box, jar, or other container to hold the slips of paper.

Directions:

Gather the children together and ask: Have you ever heard someone say, "I'm fine," and known that he or she was mad or sad or something other than "fine?" Our bodies and facial expressions almost always reveal what we are feeling, even if it's not the same as what we are saying.

Brainstorm: Ask the children to name as many words as they can that mean some level of angry. From low levels of angry, like irritate and annoy, all the way up to high levels, like furious and enraged. Record their list on chart paper. Leave the chart in place while you copy the words on slips of paper. Place the slips in a container. Have each child draw one slip of paper and pantomime the word. The children can use facial expressions, gestures, and body language, but may not say any words. Have the group guess which word (from the chart) is being acted out. Whoever guesses correctly gets to be the next person to draw a word and act it out.

Discussion Questions:

— What was it like to try to identify an angry feeling by only observing body language and facial expressions?
— What was it like to try to express an angry feeling without using your voice?
— What are some of the most obvious ways people show they are angry?

Other Things To Try:

The children can do a similar activity with partners. One child acts out one of the anger words and the partner pantomimes a positive emotion or feeling. With this variation, a list of positive words would need to be brainstormed along with the anger words. Pairs of words (one from each list) would be placed in the container.

That's What Scares Me

Art Activity

Materials:

Paper, crayons, magic markers, and/or chalk in lots of colors.

Directions:

Distribute the materials. Tell the children that they will have a chance to draw something that scares them and then get rid of the thing that scares them in a second drawing.

Explain: *We've all had bad dreams or nightmares. Think of a bad dream you have had and draw a picture of it. Put all the things in it that you can remember, especially the scary part. Then on another piece of paper, draw a picture of the same situation, but draw it so it's not scary anymore. After we finish the drawings, we'll talk about them.*

Demonstrate by drawing a picture of a nightmare that you had as a child, and then redraw it to place yourself in control. As the children work, offer suggestions to those who are having difficulty, but let them work independently.

Discussion: As they draw, praise and encourage the children for their ideas, rather than for the quality of their drawings. Ask volunteers to describe what is happening in their pictures—first the scary parts, and then how they redrew the pictures so they wouldn't have to be afraid anymore. Thank each volunteer.

Other Things To Try:

Have each child draw a picture of a scary nightmare and share it with the group. Then have the group brainstorm ways to change the picture to get rid of the scary parts.

F E A R =
False Evidence Appearing Real

Experience Sheet

Think about times when you were afraid of someone or something and everything turned out OK. There was nothing to fear after all. It was only "False Evidence Appearing Real." Make a list:

FEAR:	WHAT REALLY HAPPENED:
Example: Thought I'd failed the test	I got a B–

Can you think of a time when you got mad at someone else, but once you understood their point of view, you found you really didn't have so much to be angry about? Tell that story here:

_____
_____
_____
_____
_____
_____

160

Managing Conflict

Conflicts are an inevitable, and sometimes threatening, part of life. But there are things that we can do to turn potentially harmful conflicts into situations in which no one is hurt. This unit is designed to provide the children with non-threatening ways to explore various kinds of conflict. It also gives them opportunities to learn and practice some of the many available conflict management strategies—such as "I" messages, sharing, listening, expressing regret, putting off, compromising, negotiating, and channeling negative energy into physical activity.

I Almost Got Into a Fight

A Sharing Circle

Directions:

Introduce the topic: *Our topic for this session is, "I Almost Got Into a Fight!"*

Elaborate: *From time to time each of us has a disagreement or conflict with another person. Sometimes conflicts aren't very serious, and sometimes they are. Can you think of a time when something happened between you and someone else that almost caused you to get into a fight? Maybe you wanted to fight because you were upset. Or maybe the other person tried to start the fight. Perhaps you both felt like fighting, but then, somehow, you settled the problem peacefully. Tell us how the incident happened, and how you felt, but please don't tell us who the other person was. The topic is, "I Almost Got Into a Fight."*

Invite the children to take turns sharing. Listen carefully to each one and guide the other children to do the same. Don't allow negative interruptions. Be sure to take a turn yourself.

Discussion Questions:

After every child who wants to speak has done so, ask the children:
— Is conflict always bad, or can it sometimes lead to good things?
— What were the main ways we kept these disagreements or conflicts from becoming big fights?

How I Used an "I" Message

A Sharing Circle

Note:

This Sharing Circle should not be done until you have led the final activity, *"I" Messages Ease Tense Situations* and the concluding experience sheet, *Don't Say "You," Say "I"*.

Directions:

Introduce the topic: *Our topic for this session is, "How I Used an 'I' Message."*

Elaborate: *At our last meeting we did some skits involving "I" messages and "you" messages. Our experience sheets also covered "I" and "you" messages. Do you remember the differences between these two types of messages, and how they affect tense situations? (Discuss, as necessary.) In this Sharing Circle, we will each have a chance to tell about a time when we tried using an "I" message, and what happened when we did. If you haven't had a chance to use an "I" message yet, tell us about a time when you didn't use one, and how you think things would have turned out if you had. Tell us all about the incident, but don't tell us the names of the other people involved. Our topic is, "How I Used an 'I' Message."*

Invite the children to take turns speaking. Listen carefully to each one and guide the other children to do the same. Don't allow negative interruptions. Be sure to take a turn yourself.

Discussion Questions:

After each child who wants to speak has done so, ask the children:
— How did our "I" messages affect the people in these situations?
— How did using an "I" message make you feel about yourself?
— Why do "I" messages tend to lighten up tense situations?

Conflict Management Strategies on Stage

Drama and Discussion

Materials:

A chart showing the following conflict management strategies: 1) Sharing, 2) Listening, 3) Expressing Regret, 4) Putting Off, and 5) Compromising/Negotiating. The following conflict management scenarios, each written on a separate piece of paper:

• Two people are arguing because they both want something. They agree to share the thing they both want. (Strategy: sharing.)

• Person A is mad at person B. Person A calms down after B listens to A respectfully. (Strategy: listening.)

• Person A is upset about something. Person B expresses understanding of A's feelings and tells A that he or she is sorry that A feels so bad. (Strategy: expressing regret.)

• Two people are already feeling irritable when they start to argue about something. They agree not to say any more now, and to settle the problem later, when they both feel better. (Strategy: putting off.)

• A and B want to have different things, but they can only have one thing at a time. They agree to have some of what A wants first; then to have some of what B wants. (Strategies: compromising/negotiating.)

Directions:

Explain to the children that conflicts are an inevitable part of life, but what makes conflicts upsetting is not knowing how to handle them. If you don't know something positive to do, you may end up making matters worse. Review the Conflict Management Strategies on the chart. Give examples and ask the students to describe problems that might be resolved by each strategy.

Give the five pieces of paper with the conflict management scenarios written on them to five children, and ask each to choose a partner. Explain that each pair is to act out its conflict situation, and to demonstrate the conflict management strategy listed.

Give the children time to prepare their skits. Provide assistance, as needed.

Invite the actors to perform their skits. After each skit, ask the audience which strategy was demonstrated, and put a check mark beside it on the chart. Hold a brief discussion regarding each strategy and how well it works in managing conflict.

"I" Messages Ease Tense Situations

Drama and Discussion

Note:

This activity should be followed by the second Sharing Circle in this unit, *How I Used an "I" Message*.

Materials:

The Experience Sheets entitled, *Don't Say "You," Say "I"* (one per child).

Directions:

Begin by telling the children about two different ways that a person can respond to tense situations. A person can say, "You . . .," or a person can say "I . . ." When you start a sentence with the word **you**, it's a "you" message. When you start a sentence with the word ***I***, it's an "I" message. "You" messages often lead to blaming and name calling and can make the other person mad or hurt. They usually make a problem worse. For example: *You just took my bike without asking, you thief!* "I" messages are usually more tactful. For example: *When I discovered my bike was gone, I felt really scared. Please ask me before you use it.* "I" messages tell the other person what the problem is, how you feel about it, and what you want, or don't want, to happen.

Distribute the Experience Sheets. Tell the children to fill in the speech bubbles with "I" messages. Encourage the children to talk about what their ideas are for good "I" messages. Offer help and suggestions as needed. When the children have finished the Experience Sheets, tell them they are now going to act out the scenarios on the Experience

Sheet. Choose four volunteers to play the parts of the individuals in the two cartoons (two per cartoon).

Explain: *Plan two short skits. In the first skit, the person who is responding to the situation should get upset and deliver a "you" message to the person who spoke first. Then the two of you should keep up the negative interaction for awhile. In the second skit, the person responding to the situation should try to lighten things up by using an "I" message. We'll see how these two different ways of responding affect the people involved.*

Give the children time to plan and rehearse their skits. Then ask them to perform for the total group.

Discussion Questions:

At the end of each small group's second skit, ask the children:
— What were the effects of the "you" messages that were delivered in these skits?
— What were the effects of the "I" messages that were delivered in these skits?
— What is the benefit of using an "I" message instead of a "you" message?
— Do you think it requires some practice to learn how to use "I" messages when you're upset?
— What can you do to remember to use "I" messages in conflict situations you face in your own life?

Tell the children: *Our next Sharing Circle topic is, "How I Used an 'I' Message." So if some tense situations come up before we meet again, try using an "I" message. Then you can tell us about the situation, and how your "I" message worked.*

Don't Say "You," Say "I"
Experience Sheet

Here are two tense situations. In each one, an "I" message could be used to lighten things up. Read each situation. Draw a picture of yourself in the cartoon. Then, using an "I" message, write your response to what the other person is saying.

Situation One: You are walking down the hall. You see the biggest bullies in the school slam your friend up against a wall. Then you hear them call your friend names. You feel terrible and would like to help, but just then your friend looks at you and angrily says . . .

What do you say?

Situation Two: You borrow your older sister's bike, but while you're riding the chain falls off. You know you haven't done anything harmful to it, but when you give it back, she is very upset. She blames you by saying . . .

What do you say?

If your heart is in Social-Emotional Learning, visit us online.

Come see us at:
www.InnerchoicePublishing.com

Our website gives you a look at all our other Social-Emotional Learning-based books, free activities and learning and teaching strategies.

INNERCHOICE Publishing
15079 Oak Chase Court
Wellington, FL 33414

www.ingramcontent.com/pod-product-compliance
Lightning Source LLC
Chambersburg PA
CBHW082122230426
43671CB00015B/2782